MB

# THE POOR IN
# AMERICA

ISSUES FOR THE 90s

**MANAGING TOXIC WASTES**
by Michael Kronenwetter

**THE POOR IN AMERICA**
by Suzanne M. Coil

**THE WAR ON TERRORISM**
by Michael Kronenwetter

ISSUES FOR THE 90s

# THE POOR IN AMERICA

Suzanne M. Coil

**JULIAN MESSNER**

JULIAN MESSNER and colophon are trademarks of
Simon & Schuster, Inc. Design by Claire Counihan.
Manufactured in the United States of America.

Lib. ed. 10 9 8 7 6 5 4 3 2 1

**Library of Congress Cataloging-in-Publication Data**

Coil, Suzanne M.
The poor in America / Suzanne M. Coil.
p.   cm.—(Issues for the 90s)
Bibliography:  p.
Includes index.
Summary: Discusses poverty in the past, present, and future,
and those whom it affects.
1. Poor—United States—Juvenile literature.   [1. Poor.
2. Poverty.]   I. Title.   II. Series.
HC110.P6C55   1989
362.5'0973—dc20                    89-12116
ISBN 0-671-69052-3                 CIP
                                   AC

# DEDICATION

This book is for my grandparents, Karl Armbrust (1865-1933) and Magdalena Ertl Armbrust (1866-1924), and for my parents, Magdalena Armbrust Wolf and Michael Wolf, whose hard passage landed them on Ellis Island, and who made themselves a new home in America; and this book is for my son René Coil, and for my daughter Astrid and her husband Keith Lenox, and for my grandson Christopher Lenox. But especially, this book is for my husband Jesse, whose forefathers made the long journey from England in the early 1700s to till the green fields of Virginia until the mysteries behind the mountains lured them west.

# CONTENTS

ONE **THE FACE OF POVERTY**                                1

TWO **POVERTY IN THE NATION'S PAST**                      8

THREE **POVERTY IN THE TWENTIETH CENTURY**              17

FOUR **POVERTY TODAY**                                   32

FIVE **THE CHRONIC POOR**                                44

SIX **WOMEN AND CHILDREN**                               65

SEVEN **THE ELDERLY**                                    76

EIGHT **THE NEW POOR**                                   86

NINE **POVERTY—CHALLENGES FOR THE 1990S**               97

BIBLIOGRAPHY    115

INDEX    121

# THE POOR IN
# AMERICA

# CHAPTER ONE

# THE FACE OF

# POVERTY

"**M**ONEY can't buy happiness" is a common saying. People usually agree, though, that it is easier to have a more comfortable and fulfilling life with money than without it. Without money, we could not pay for such basic needs as food, shelter, clothing, health care, and transportation. Nor could we have other things many people value, such as a college education or vacation.

Most Americans enjoy a comfortable standard of living. The "American dream" suggests that anyone can prosper by working hard toward a goal. For many, the "dream" becomes reality as hard work and planning result in a prosperous life for themselves and their families.

Statistics released by the U.S. Bureau of the Census confirm that the majority of American families have incomes sufficient for their needs. In 1985, the median income for a four-person family with one wage earner was about $28,000 per year. In families with two wage earners (about 42 percent), the median income was close to $32,000. (Median income means that half of the families had a higher income and half had a lower income.) Twenty percent had incomes above $50,000, while the top 1 percent earned $150,000 or more.

Things that Americans often take for granted are considered luxuries by people in some other countries. Most Americans own a car. Many own their homes, complete with indoor plumbing, electricity, telephones, air-conditioning, and a variety of labor-saving devices such as washing machines and lawn mowers. Ninety-eight percent of American homes contain at least one television set; 34 percent contain videocassette recorders (VCRs). About 7 percent have at least one compact disc player, and sales of this electronic wonder are rising steadily. To the majority of people in the world, the average American home holds undreamed-of riches.

Yet not everyone in the United States is prosperous or even adequately fed. The ugly problem of poverty is frequently discussed in newspapers, books and magazines, and on television. Despite the power and plenty associated with the United States, a large number of Americans are poor. They include young and old, blacks, whites, Hispanics, and native Americans. A disproportionate number are women and children.

For these people, life is a daily struggle. Often, they do not have enough food—or enough quality food—to maintain good health. They may be unemployed or employed in low-salary jobs that do not pay for their basic needs. Some are too sick or disabled to support themselves. They live in rural areas, as well as crowded cities and in all regions of the country. Some— perhaps as many as 3 million people—have no homes.

## MEASURING POVERTY

How many Americans are poor? No one knows exactly, but every year, the U.S. Census Bureau estimates how many people have incomes below the government's official poverty line.

The stark contrast between affluence and poverty can be seen in many places in American cities. Reuters/Bettmann Newsphotos

Government economists look at current prices for food, housing, and other necessities, then determine the minimum amount of money the "average person" needs in order to buy these things. People whose incomes fall below that minimum amount—or poverty line—are considered officially poor.

The September 1988 Census Bureau report, based on a 1987 survey, showed that nearly 33 million people—about 13.5 percent of the population—live at or below the official poverty line.

However, many people contend that the government's figures are too low. Michael Harrington, author of *The Other America* and *The New American Poverty,* argues that official calculations have been "profoundly understating" the number of poor people in this country. Poverty is more widespread and may include more than 20 percent of the population, says Harrington.

Why such a difference in these estimates of the number of people living in poverty? One reason is the method used to define poverty. The federal government bases its definition on a study conducted by the Department of Agriculture in 1955, which said that the average American family spends one-third of its after-tax income on food. The remainder of a family's income, said the study, is spent on such things as housing, clothing, health care, education, transportation, and other expenses.

Using the cost of an "economy food budget" developed by the U.S. Department of Agriculture, the government then multiplied the food budget cost by three, because food was assumed to cost one-third of the family's income. The economy food budget included the smallest amounts of the various foods needed to meet minimum nutritional needs.

Critics contend that the government's definition of poverty is unrealistic. It looks at before-tax income, not the cash people have in hand after paying taxes. Also, it does not consider the fact that costs for housing, transportation, health care, and other items and services vary widely in different parts of the country. Recent surveys show that Americans now spend closer to 20 percent—(one-fifth)—of their income on food, not one-third. This means we would have to multiply the economy food budget by five, not three, to reach a more accurate poverty level figure. As a result, many more Americans would fall within the official definition of poverty.

For example, using the government's guidelines, a family of four with an income of $11,611 in 1987 was living in poverty. One-third of that—the economy food budget figure—is about $3,870 (what the family would need that year to buy food). Thus, $7,741 would be left to pay the family's remaining expenses during the year: taxes, housing, fuel, utilities, clothing, medical and dental care, transportation, education, household utensils, supplies and repairs, and other items. Dividing $7,741 by twelve gives the family $645 a month to buy these nonfood items. In many parts of the country, *housing costs alone* could absorb this amount of money, leaving nothing for other essentials. If the 1987 economy food budget figure were multiplied by five, the revised poverty level income would be $19,350 for a family of four.

The number of the "official poor" increases greatly if this revised formula is used. In addition, some people, such as undocumented workers and the homeless, are not currently included in the statistics. Including these people raises the numbers even more.

## BROADER DEFINITIONS OF POVERTY

These statistics are only numbers and don't describe what it is like to be poor. Most definitions of poverty focus on economic deprivation—that being poor means lacking enough money or other resources to secure the basic needs of life on an ongoing basis. Is poverty really just a matter of low income? In his book, *Poverty in the United Kingdom*, British sociologist Peter Townsend defines poverty as "the lack of resources necessary to permit participation in the activities, customs, and diets commonly approved by society." This broadens the definition of poverty to include a sense of "relative deprivation"—the feeling that one is disadvantaged in comparison with other people in the

environment. Without enough money, people can't afford a good
education, legal services, or vacations; they can't eat out in
restaurants or take their children to the movies. When they do
participate in certain activities or venture out of their neighborhoods, they may be treated as less important than those with a
higher social and economic status.

Thus, poverty is not just a matter of income. It means a lack
of certain social and cultural advantages, as well as material
things. It may involve "low wages and chronic employment and
underemployment, lack of property ownership, absence of
savings, absence of food reserves in the home, and a chronic
shortage of cash [which] reduce the possibility of effective
participation in the larger economic system," according to
anthropologist Oscar Lewis, who made extensive studies of
poverty.

The number of poor in the United States is between 33 and
50 million, depending upon who is counting and what method is
used. Behind those statistics are real people. Who are they?

Many of the poor are children. The U.S. Census Bureau
estimates that one child in five—20 percent of American
children—lives in poverty.

Many of the poor are women. Nearly three of every ten
households headed by white women and more than half of all
households headed by black women have incomes below the
poverty line.

Poverty afflicts the elderly. For those who have suffered from
ill health or whose low-paying jobs gave them no chance to save,
Social Security benefits alone may not pay for necessities.
Among the nation's elderly, black citizens are particularly
disadvantaged: Nearly one-third of all elderly blacks lives on less
than $5,300 a year. The figure is even higher—55 percent—for
elderly black women living alone.

Indeed, statistics from the Bureau of the Census show that
poverty is increasing: The national poverty rate in 1986 (13.6
percent) was higher than in any year from 1969 through 1980,
having reached 14.4 percent in 1984. Among these statistics are

people called the "new poor": growing numbers of displaced industrial workers, farm families, and the homeless. The National Coalition for the Homeless estimates that there may be as many as 3 million people who are homeless. In New York City, about 30,000 homeless people, including children, crowd the public shelters or seek refuge in railroad stations, bus terminals, parks, or makeshift shelters on the streets.

These, then, are some of the definitions and statistics that outline the problem of poverty in the United States. The following chapters will describe the faces behind these statistics and explore some important questions:

- Why does poverty exist in a land of power and plenty? What causes it?

- Who are the "poor" and where and how do they live? Have they always been poor? If not, how did they become disadvantaged? What is it like to be poor—what are the effects of hunger and malnutrition, inadequate housing, lack of education and illiteracy, unemployment?

- How does poverty affect society as a whole? How do the government's social and economic policies affect the poor? What roles can the government and private sector play in preventing and alleviating poverty?

Before we address these important issues, we will examine the history of poverty in the United States—its existence since colonial times and the various methods used to prevent and alleviate it.

CHAPTER TWO

# POVERTY IN

# THE NATION'S PAST

**W**HEN the early colonists arrived in the New World, they found a vast continent rich in natural resources. Settling in the New World involved a strenuous ocean voyage and uncertain future, but people took such risks in order to gain religious and political freedoms and the opportunity to improve their economic and social status.

Poverty in their homelands prompted most people to sail to the New World. A handbill advertising for colonists in 1630 read:

In England land scarce and labour plenty
In Virginia land free and labour scarce.

People who wanted to go to the New World but lacked the money to pay for the voyage could become *indentured servants*. They pledged to work without pay for an agreed-upon length of time—usually three to seven years—in exchange for their passage. The fate of these unpaid workers depended upon the kind of treatment they received from their masters. When their servitude ended, they received a few possessions, such as clothing, a gun, and a few acres of land.

# THE INSTITUTION OF SLAVERY

The demand for inexpensive labor in the colonies grew, yet there were not enough indentured servants to satisfy it. Nonindentured men often chose to start their own farms or businesses instead of working for others.

In response to this labor shortage, black Africans were brought to America as slaves. During the seventeenth and eighteenth centuries, European countries were still buying and selling slaves. Slave traders from England and the colonies seized black people from their homeland in Africa then sold them in the New World. From these black slaves, a master could demand a lifetime of work. If the slave had children, the master owned them, too, thereby increasing his source of labor.

Thus began the institutionalization of slavery, a shameful chapter in American history. Some slaves were freed; others were treated "fairly" by their masters. Most lived with poverty, hard labor, disrupted families, and a lack of education. Many people thought slavery was wrong and tried to abolish it, but so great was the desire for workers, especially on the large southern plantations, that slavery continued. Slavery and its aftermath of racism, poll taxes, and separate-but-not-equal facilities have had a serious impact on the poverty still experienced by disproportionate numbers of black Americans.

Other colonists experienced poverty, too. A small farmer's livelihood might be shattered by bad weather or a plague of insects. Farmers often relied on credit to buy the tools they needed, but if crop prices fell, they could not repay their loans.

On the other hand, many colonists prospered. In Virginia, for example, tobacco growers could sell their crops in England for a high price. Cotton, furs, lumber, and other products also could be profitably sold in Europe.

How did the more affluent colonists respond to the problem of poverty? Those perceived as helpless—orphans, widows, the aged, the disabled—were given cash or material goods or they might be boarded at the town's expense. Shelters and public hospitals took care of those who could not care for themselves. Often, the people who extended charity were motivated by their religious beliefs.

Those who were seen as able-bodied but unwilling to work were regarded much less favorably. Debtors were often imprisoned. Unemployed paupers were whipped, imprisoned, and even sold into temporary servitude at public auctions. In 1697, a colonial court sold thirty-three orphan children into servitude to prevent them from becoming "idlers." During the early 1700s, some towns established workhouses where the indigent were forced to work.

## THE "HOLY EXPERIMENT"

In 1682, the ship *Welcome* brought William Penn and some other members of his religious group, the Society of Friends, to the land now known as Pennsylvania. Seeking freedom of worship, they regarded their colony as a "holy experiment" and hoped it would embody their ideals of love, peace, and brotherhood.

The Friends—or Quakers—believed that the wealthy should share their worldly goods with the needy. People were expected to live simply, wasting nothing, and, as William Penn said, "clothe the naked and feed the hungry from what is left over."

In Penn's colony, steps were taken to ensure that no one lacked food, clothing, shelter, or fuel. Jobs were provided for the unemployed. If someone's house burned, money was collected to rebuild it. Medical care was provided for the sick. Help was given not only to fellow Quakers but to anyone in need. Debtors were not imprisoned for small debts, as they were in other colonies. Prisons became "workshops" where prisoners could learn a useful trade and be guided toward less anti-social conduct.

The Quakers also believed in the value of education. Parents were required by law to make sure all their children learned to read and write. All boys, rich or poor, had to learn a trade in order to earn a living, if that became necessary.

The holy experiment continued for more than seventy years, but as time passed, disputes among different leaders arose and the colony's population became larger and more diverse. The ideals that guided the original colony changed and the experiment ended.

## AFTER THE REVOLUTION

"The spirit of enthusiasm which overcame everything at first is now done with," said George Washington, describing the mood of his troops at the end of the American Revolution in 1783. That war, which freed the colonists from the economic and political grip of England, resulted in wide variations in the conditions of the new Americans. Many volunteer soldiers found themselves poor. The new government was in debt, and the millions of dollars in paper currency issued by the Constitutional Congress became worthless as inflation mounted.

The leaders of the new nation had to confront such major issues as slavery, education, the vote, the economy, and landlessness. Thomas Jefferson expressed the hope that the new nation would prosper as a nation of small farmers. He suggested that "every person of full age...be entitled to an appropriation of fifty acres."

One result of the American Revolution was that more land became available. Within the territory that had made up the thirteen colonies, the government confiscated lands of those who had supported England during the war, then divided these lands into smaller farms that were sold at auction. More important was the opening of lands west of the Allegheny Mountains. England had banned the colonists from settling the area that extended from the mountains to the Mississippi River and from the Great Lakes to west Florida. Now that the colonies had defeated England, the new nation could expand in earnest. By 1790, more than 220,000 pioneers had established new homes west of the mountains.

The increased availability of land helped many who were living in poverty. However, several key reforms proposed by Jefferson and others—the abolition of imprisonment for debt, the right to vote without owning property, free public education, and the abolition of slavery—were left unresolved until the 1800s.

## THE NINETEENTH CENTURY

While the American Revolution was being fought on one continent, another revolution was taking place in England. With the invention of the spinning jenny in 1764, the Industrial Revolution had begun. Labor-saving machines powered by water and steam, and later by coal and electricity, were to change all aspects of society. One result of the new machines was the factory-filled cities that sheltered new forms of poverty.

Thomas Jefferson, who had watched women and children laboring long hours in English factories, was among those who disliked the system. Speaking of factory owners, he said, "I consider the class of artificers as the panders of vice and the instruments by which the liberties of a country are generally overturned."

Other Americans, however, such as Alexander Hamilton, argued that factories would provide jobs for the idle, stimulate the demand for raw materials, and encourage immigration. He commented that by working in factories, the children "are rendered...more early useful by manufacturing establishments than they would otherwise be." Hamilton and his supporters encouraged the establishment of manufacturing by making investment capital and credit available to entrepreneurs and by placing high taxes on imported goods.

The number of factories in the United States rose steadily. By 1830, 795 cotton mills were operating in the United States; by the outbreak of the Civil War in 1860, more than 1.3 million workers were employed by the country's 140,000 manufacturing and industrial plants.

Immigrants came in ever-increasing numbers to fill the need for cheap labor in the factories and to help construct roads, canals, and railroads.

Many urban workers endured terrible conditions both at work and at home. The factories were often unsafe and unsanitary. The crowded tenements lacked light, ventilation, water, and sanitation. Frequently, several families shared a single room infested with vermin and rats. Families often subsisted on meager diets of potatoes, bread, and cabbage. Water had to be drawn from outside hydrants, sewage systems were inadequate or even nonexistent, and garbage rotted in the streets. Diseases such as typhoid fever, influenza, tuberculosis, and cholera were common. Crime and drunkenness increased. Women and girls, whose wages were typically less than half those of men, often begged, stole, or resorted to prostitution to stay alive. Infant mortality was high, and children suffered from lack of adequate food and shelter. In 1852, for example, the New York City police reported that 10,000 homeless children were living in the streets.

Writing in the *New York Tribune* in 1851, Horace Greeley urged people to "fly, scatter through the country, go to the Great West, anything but stay here." He estimated that a family of five needed $10.57 a week in order to buy the barest necessities. Yet workmen were earning as little as sixty-nine cents for a twelve-and-a-half-hour day of exhausting labor.

Throughout the remainder of the nineteenth century, poverty or the threat of poverty haunted the working class. Fluctuations in the economy periodically plunged the nation into depression, and the ordinary worker had little control over these events.

Relief for the poor came primarily from charitable organizations formed by private citizens and from local governments. Soup kitchens, handouts of clothing, orphan societies, and other forms of charity gave some help to those in need.

Some significant steps were also taken by the government. By 1860, imprisonment for debt was abolished. The right to vote was extended to all white males without regard to property or wealth. Slowly, the country moved toward a system of free, compulsory education.

Many workers united to ask for land to start family farms. Through George Henry Evans' National Reform Association, popularly called the "Vote Yourself a Farm" movement, workers urged legislators to release more public lands. One result of their efforts was the Homestead Act of 1862, which by 1890 made 48 million acres available.

Slavery was finally abolished in 1863 after decades of protest and a long, bitter war. When the Civil War ended in 1865, 4 million former slaves were "free" to start over as best they could. Concerned that something should be done to help them, Thaddeus Stevens, a congressman from Pennsylvania, said, "We have turned...loose four million slaves without a hut to shelter them or a cent in their pockets. The infernal laws of slavery have prevented them from acquiring an education, understanding the common laws of contract, or of managing the ordinary business of life." Stevens recommended that each black family receive forty acres of free land and $50 in cash.

Congress did provide some protection for the ex-slaves. It passed the Civil Rights Act, which promised them legal equality; the Freedmen's Act, which provided some emergency relief; and the Fourteenth Amendment to the Constitution, which conferred full citizenship on blacks. The Freedmen's Bureau established hospitals and schools, and millions of food packets were distributed (one-fourth of them to poor whites). Thousands of labor contracts were arranged.

Stevens' proposal to give the former slaves forty acres of free land was never enacted. Fifty years after emancipation, three-fourths of all black farmers were working as sharecroppers or tenant farmers on land owned by whites. More than half of the nation's blacks were illiterate and one-third were employed as servants.

Despite many problems, the years between 1860 and 1890 were years of unprecedented prosperity for the nation as a whole. While the population doubled, wealth quadrupled and industrial output increased 500 percent.

Following the Civil War, as we have seen, thousands of pioneers took advantage of the Homestead Act and moved westward. A man could be granted 160 acres of land free if he lived there for five years and settled a farm (homestead) on the grant. By using such new machines as combines, seeders, and reapers, he could hope to double his production of grain. Between 1860 and 1900, the number of U.S. farms grew from 2 million to almost 6 million. The amount of land under cultivation doubled—from 400 million acres to 800 million. By 1900, more than 200,000 miles of railroad track had been laid across the country, making it easier to transport farm products.

Nevertheless, frontier farmers faced numerous difficulties. In addition to long hours of toil, they endured isolation, floods, blizzards, plaques of insects, dust storms, prairie fires, drought, and stampeding buffalo. There were other problems, too— namely, railroaders, banks, and landboomers.

In the course of building the transcontinental railroad, the railroad companies and speculators had secured title, either legitimately or through fraud, to half a billion acres of land. Through powerful advertising campaigns, they encouraged thousands of people to buy land from them on credit. In order to repay their loans, these people worked from sunup to sundown to clear the land, plant seeds, and harvest crops.

As a result, there was an overproduction of crops, which drove prices down. In 1869 the price of corn was seventy-five cents a bushel, but by 1869, the price had dropped to twenty-eight cents. Other crops suffered similar drops in price. Additionally, the crops became totally worthless if the farmer could not get them to market. For that, he needed the railroads.

Because the railroads had a monopoly on shipping, they could charge whatever price they chose. In 1869, when corn was selling for seventy-five cents a bushel in the East, the railroads charged

Life for these homesteaders in Washington Territory around 1890 lacked many of the amenities Americans take for granted today. The Bettmann Archive, Inc.

fifty-three cents to ship it from Iowa. Thus, the farmer received only twenty-two cents for all his investment and labor.

As a result of such problems, many farmers incurred large debts, and rural poverty became widespread. An orator of that time suggested that the farmers should "raise less corn and more hell."

Groups of farmers united in a variety of economic and political organizations and eventually formed the People's Party. Known as the Populist movement, this party fought for reforms that would protect farmers from poverty. It challenged the notion that "government is best that governs least" and asked Americans to take a new look at the role and responsibility of government. The Populists maintained that the government should regulate commerce and industry, control and protect the money supply, and protect the rights of common people who, it said, were often victims of "class legislation and favoritism."

By bringing these issues before the nation, the rural poor of the Populist era paved the way for greater government involvement in the plight of the poor in the twentieth century.

# CHAPTER THREE

# POVERTY IN THE

# TWENTIETH CENTURY

**A**T the turn of the century, elaborate mansions lined the fashionable avenues of New York, Chicago, and other cities. Their residents included millionaires like William K. Vanderbilt, the railroad tycoon whose wife once gave a party that cost $250,000, and Andrew Carnegie of Pittsburgh, the Scottish immigrant who worked his way to the top of the steel industry and during one year (1900) earned $23 million.

During the same period, millions of unemployed people depended upon the food they received in breadlines to avoid starvation. The contrast between the very rich and the very poor was starkly drawn when newspapers reported that a society matron had paid $10,000 for a gold dress, while pleas for relief by a conference of labor union delegates went unanswered by the government.

After 1900, the wealthy class continued to grow. At the same time, between 1900 and the start of World War I in 1917, farm incomes rose and a growing middle class enjoyed greater prosperity. More than 2 million skilled workers improved their economic situation greatly by organizing trade unions under the American Federation of Labor.

As industry and commerce grew, however, the United States had shifted from a rural to an urban economy. Within many cities, poverty reached alarming proportions. Between 1900 and 1915, more than 13 million immigrants, most of them from southern and eastern Europe, came to America. Needing to work, they accepted low-paying factory and laborers' jobs and rented lodgings in overcrowded slums.

A number of people, dismayed by conditions in the slums, determined to bring the plight of the poor to the attention of other citizens. Numerous books and articles were published about the condition of the working class. Among the most influential of these books were those written by journalist-photographer Jacob Riis, a Danish-born New Yorker. Called the "emancipator of the slums," Riis documented the grim conditions he observed with photographs as well as with words in such books as *How the Other Half Lives* (1890) and *The Children of the Tenements* (1904). Riis' depiction of life in the New York slums roused many Americans, including the future president, Theodore Roosevelt, who called him "the most useful American of his day." Writers Lincoln Steffens and Robert Hunter were among others who called for reforms, including slum clearance, child labor laws, sanitation, health care, and more regulation of "sweatshops."

The nation's attention was increasingly drawn to conditions in the sweatshops. Industrial accidents caused numerous deaths and injuries. In 1908 alone, 35,000 laborers were killed on the job. Occupational diseases such as lead poisoning and chronic lung infections disabled thousands more. In 1911, a fire at the Triangle Shirtwaist Company claimed the lives of 145 workers, mostly young girls.

This immigrant family, living in a squalid tenement bedroom, was typical of many who filled the slums of New York and other cities in the early 1900s. The Bettmann Archive, Inc.

Workers themselves fought for better working conditions and higher wages. There were 4,000 organized strikes and walkouts in 1903 alone, but the cost of these protests was often high. For example, forty-two workers were killed during a miners' strike in Cripple Creek, Colorado.

Fueled by the increasing dissent of the workers along with

continuing efforts by writers, social workers, concerned citizens, and politicans, the "reform" movement progressed. These people were convinced that the government should take more responsibility for the problem of poverty. When President Theodore Roosevelt entered the White House, the federal government instituted a series of "trust busting" and regulatory actions that limited the powers of the giant corporations. State and local governments passed laws governing the minimum age at which minors could be employed and the maximum number of hours that minors and females could work. Workmen's compensation bills gave protection to those who were injured in the workplace.

More "social legislation" followed. At his 1912 inauguration, President Woodrow Wilson said,

> We have been proud of our industrial achievements but we have not hitherto stopped thoughtfully enough to count the human cost, the cost of lives snuffed out, of energies overtaxed and broken, the fearful physical and spiritual cost to the men and women and children upon whom the dead weight and burden of it all has fallen pitilessly the years through.

During Wilson's administration, the powers of large corporations and banks were further limited by new laws and by the institution of regulatory agencies such as the Federal Reserve Board and the Federal Trade Commission. Farmers could obtain easier credit, and government employees were covered by a new workmen's compensation law. These measures curbed the powers of monopolies and corporations but did not solve all the problems of poverty.

## THE ROARING TWENTIES

When World War I ended in 1918, a spirited optimism took hold in the United States. Technology was developing rapidly. All kinds of "new-fangled" contraptions—automobiles, radios, electrical appliances, telephones—were available. People were even flying in airplanes!

The 1920s promised to be a prosperous age. Many citizens seemed to go on a "spending spree," purchasing the new consumer goods on the installment plan and investing surplus funds in bank accounts, real estate schemes, and in that wonderful moneymaking machine, the stock market. President Calvin Coolidge announced in 1925 that "the business of America is business," and business was booming.

Many things seemed possible, even the elimination of poverty. Herbert Hoover proclaimed in 1928 that "We are nearer to the final triumph over poverty than ever before." Indeed, between the years 1900 and 1929, the number of poor declined from about 14 million to 4 million.

Beneath the surface, however, the economy showed signs of trouble. At the height of the "boom," 19 percent of the country's factories were idle, and 2 million workers were unemployed. Overproduction had sent farm prices lower, and nearly 2 million farmers left the land. Many people who invested in the stock market did so by borrowing up to 90 percent of the money "on margin." According to the Brookings Institution, a Washington, D.C.–based organization that analyzes statistics and economic trends, a family of four needed $2,000 per year to buy "only basic necessities." Sixty percent of the population was earning just that amount or less.

These were just a few of the problems that proceeded the stock market crash of 1929, beginning a series of devastating events known as the "Great Depression."

## THE GREAT DEPRESSION

On "Black Thursday," October 24, 1929, the bubble burst. Prices on the New York Stock Exchange plummeted. Speculation buying had pushed some of the prices higher than what the companies were actually worth. As stock prices plunged, shareholders tried to sell, but nobody was buying. Many stock owners who had borrowed money for their purchases could not repay their debts. If they had pledged their homes or other possessions as "collateral" to borrow money, then they had to surrender those possessions.

The economy collapsed. Despite frantic maneuvers by financiers and politicians, conditions deteriorated. Over the next several years, nearly 5,000 banks closed, and the depositors lost their life savings. Thousands of businesses declared bankruptcy because consumers could no longer afford to buy their products. By early 1933, nearly 17 million people had lost their jobs. Those who still had jobs were working for drastically reduced wages. Farm prices plunged as well, and lending institutions foreclosed on farm and home mortgages.

Hunger and homelessness were widespread. Soup kitchens and breadlines distributed food to increasingly long lines of people. Other hungry people rummaged through garbage cans looking for something to eat. According to the U.S. Department of Labor, nearly 200,000 abandoned or homeless children roamed the country, begging or stealing to survive. More than 1 million people lived in huts made of cardboard or discarded tin in shanty towns sarcastically called "Hoovervilles," after the president, who many people blamed for their troubles. Thousands of men stowed away on freight trains, crisscrossing the country in search of work.

Although people were starving, a number of farmers burned their crops when they could not afford to ship them to market. Some even had to slaughter their livestock because they could not afford to buy feed. Dust storms and foreclosures drove thousands of farmers off the land.

President Hoover opposed a system of national relief. He believed that the way out of the depression was to rebuild industry and commerce, which would, in turn, create jobs. He hoped that people would help the needy with volunteer charity through such programs as the Organization for Unemployment Relief, which encouraged the sharing of food.

Many people protested the government's policies. One of the most public of these protests occurred on July 28, 1932, when several thousand unemployed World War I veterans gathered in the nation's capital to urge Congress to pay all veterans a cash bonus of $1,000 in recognition of their wartime service. The "Bonus March" received much attention, but Congress opposed the bill two days later.

The country elected a new leader, Franklin Delano Roosevelt. In his famous 1932 inaugural address, President Roosevelt announced that one third of the nation was "ill-clothed, ill-housed and ill-fed." He pledged a "New Deal" for the American people and proceeded with rapid changes. During the first hundred days of the Roosevelt administration, more legislation was enacted and more executive actions were taken than at any other time in history.

The president called on a group of experts, nicknamed the "brain trust," to provide immediate solutions to the nation's urgent problems.

Harry L. Hopkins, one of the "brains," was asked to confront the pressing problems of hunger and unemployment. Hopkins believed that millions of Americans had been reduced to poverty by factors beyond their control and that the government should give them direct cash assistance. Soon, relief funds were bringing help to 28 million people.

Hopkins also reasoned that most people wanted jobs, not a "handout." Under his supervision, the Civil Works administration created 4 million temporary jobs in 180,000 work projects around the country. The Public Works Administration (PWA), another Hopkins "brain child," stimulated the construction industry. Thousands of hospitals, schools, auditoriums, and other public buildings were constructed. The Tennessee Valley Authority irrigation and reclamation project, tunnels, bridges, dams, thousands of miles of highways, and a host of other useful projects were all part of the PWA program. Altogether, the PWA spent $4 billion on 34,000 construction projects and created 500,000 jobs.

Another program—the Civilian Conservation Corps—gave employment and military training to 2.5 million teenagers. CCC volunteers lived in camps where they performed various kinds of work and were paid $30 a month, most of which they were expected to send home to their families.

Providing money for those in desperate need and creating jobs solved only a part of the problem, however. Ways had to be found to help industry and agriculture recover. Just how to achieve this was the subject of much controversy. On one side were those who insisted that it was necessary to break up the large corporate monopolies that competed unfairly with small businesses. Government, they said, should enact anti-trust legislation, as well as reform and welfare measures to protect the "little man." On the other side were the "planners" who believed that government should take a larger hand in regulating and controlling industry and agriculture.

The National Industrial Recovery Act of 1933 (which was later declared unconstitutional) reflected the views of the "planners." The Act called for measures that would organize business enterprises, increase employment, stimulate production, and generate economic activity. Industry representatives were given the power to fix prices and to adjust supply to demand. The Securities and Exchange Commission was formed to prevent excesses in stock market speculation.

At the same time that the government was trying to regulate business and industry, it also acted to help workers. In response to increased labor unrest and violent strikes, Congress passed laws that empowered labor unions to bargain for better working conditions and wages and set guidelines for this collective bargaining between workers and employers. To protect millions of workers who did not belong to unions, new laws set standards for both hours and wages in many industries, especially those characterized by low wages and long hours. The forty-hour work week was made standard, child labor was abolished, and the first minimum wage was set at twenty-five cents an hour.

Farmers also benefited from the government's intervention. During the depression, much as in an earlier time, farmers were starving and being evicted from the land not because they produced too little but because they produced too much. To bring the system into balance, the government paid farmers to plant fewer crops, purchased and stockpiled surpluses, set production quotas and "parity" prices, and made easy-credit loans available.

Other New Deal legislation attacked a variety of problems. The Social Security Act of 1935, one of the most important pieces of social legislation ever enacted in the United States, provided certain classes of workers with unemployment insurance, old age benefits, and assistance to dependent mothers and children and to those suffering from poverty, blindness, and other disabilities. The Works Progress Administration (WPA) gave jobs to more than 8 million people. Bridges, airports, roads, sewage systems, and more than 110,000 schools, libraries, hospitals, and other structures were built.

Despite these major government efforts and the expenditure of billions of dollars, poverty continued to afflict the nation. At the end of 1938, there were still 11 million people unemployed. In the end, it was war, not legislation, that brought an end to the depression.

Across the Atlantic, with Germany's invasion of Poland in 1939, World War II was under way. It was orders from the United States' allies for military equipment that finally shifted American industry into high gear and provided much-needed jobs. When the United States entered the war in 1941, factories began to operate at full capacity, and the economy forged ahead.

Although the New Deal failed to eradicate poverty, it did bring much-needed relief to many people, and its legislation (such as the Social Security Act) established a basis for future social programs. The New Deal also addressed the question of a government's responsibility for the welfare of its citizens. The Great Depression had played havoc with the American dream. Even though they had spent their lives working hard, millions of Americans lost everything they owned. Millions experienced hunger and deprivation, and many felt that their destinies were ruled by complex economic forces beyond their control. In response to the extreme needs of Americans during the depression, government officials as well as many private citizens came to see poverty as no longer the concern of just the afflicted individual. Handouts, soup kitchens, private charity—these had not been enough. Society at large had been forced to respond.

## THE WAR ON POVERTY

The nation's attention was focused on other pressing issues during and immediately after World War II, and the problem of poverty took a back seat. As a growing middle class was enjoying unparalleled prosperity, the poor became somewhat "invisible," although their numbers were still large. Studies conducted during the 1950s showed that 20 percent of American families were surviving on less than $1,500 a year, and a large percentage of them were black.

During the 1940s and 1950s, nearly 3 million black Americans left the rural South to seek jobs in northern and western manufacturing centers. They crowded into ghettos of Detroit, Chicago, New York, Los Angeles, and other cities. Their unemployment rate was more than twice as high as that of whites, and their incomes were only half as much. Black unemployment was a severe problem, and the lack of social and political equality had negative consequences on other areas of life as well.

In December 1955, an unknown black woman in Montgomery, Alabama, became a pivotal figure in the growing social protest against inequality. Mrs. Rosa Parks, riding home on the bus after a long day at work, refused to surrender her seat to a white man, and she was arrested. The word spread—"Don't ride the bus on Monday!"—as the city's 17,000 black residents began a successful boycott to protest segregation and the second-class treatment of blacks. The Montgomery bus boycott, which lasted throughout 1956, was only one of many such protests as the civil rights movement got under way, forcing the United States to consider the injustices suffered by many of its citizens.

When John F. Kennedy became president in 1960, the movement had gained momentum. Sensitive to the growing concern about social and economic justice, Kennedy said, "If a free society cannot help the many who are poor, it cannot save the few who are rich." The president agreed with a 1959 report by the Conference on Economic Progress that proposed a $23.5 billion increase in the national budget to provide various kinds of help for Americans living in poverty or deprivation. He urged Congress to act on a range of problems including inadequate education, cities "engulfed in squalor," deficiencies in health care, pollution, and low-income housing. Believing that the responsibility for change did not rest only with government, Kennedy exhorted citizens: "Ask not what your country can do for you, ask what you can do for your country."

Civil rights activists were encouraged by Kennedy's vocal support of their cause. They continued to concentrate on the problem of segregation in the South, as well as on voting rights. The focus broadened to include equality in jobs and income. In 1963, 200,000 blacks and whites joined in the "March on Washington for Freedom and Jobs."

While Martin Luther King, Jr., and other leaders and civil rights workers marched and demonstrated, Michael Harrington attacked poverty in his book, *The Other America*. Harrington presented vivid and moving portrayals of the day-to-day struggles of the poor in this country. "To be impoverished," he wrote, "is to be an internal alien, to grow up in a culture that is radically different from the one that dominates society." Harrington maintained that the nation's prosperity was not trickling down to the needy at the bottom of society and urged that the larger society use "its help and resources...to really make it possible for these people to help themselves."

President Kennedy was one of the people influenced by Harrington's book. He called on the Council of Economic Advisors to devise a plan for those in need. Kennedy intended to announce the plan during his next message to Congress, but his life was cut short by an assassin's bullet on November 22, 1963. It was up to the next president Lyndon B. Johnson, to continue.

After only five days in office, Johnson urged the passage of a civil rights law. A few weeks later, in his State of the Union speech, he deplored the fact that

> ...many Americans live on the outskirts of hope, some because of their poverty and some because of their color, and all too many because of both. Our task is to help reduce their despair with opportunity. And this administration today, here and now, declares unconditional war on poverty in America....

Johnson's Great Society programs included the Medicare-Social Security Bill of 1965 that provided medical, hospital, and nursing care coverage for the elderly, an aid to education law that allocated roughly $1 billion to school districts serving poor children, and the Higher Education Act, which made billions of dollars available for college student loans and adult education programs. Additional legislation outlawed poll taxes and literacy tests for voters, both of which had been used to prevent minority citizens from exercising their right to vote.

Perhaps the most far-reaching piece of legislation, passed by Congress in 1966, was the Economic Opportunity Act, popularly called the "anti-poverty law." Its aim was to help people break the cycle of poverty by helping them to acquire the training and skills necessary to get a job. As Vice President Hubert Humphrey pointed out, "education holds the key to escape from the mire of poverty." Under the provisions of this law, hundreds of thousands of young people, low-income college students, and school dropouts were enrolled in various types of "work training" and "work study" programs that made it possible for them to continue their educations.

Community action programs made up the second major part of the "anti-poverty" bill. These included such programs as Operation Head Start (which successfully enrolled 750,000 children in preschool programs), health centers, legal aid to the poor, loans to small businesses and farmers, and help to migrants and Indians.

Additional Great Society legislation called for a massive public housing program, public works projects in the economically depressed Appalachian region, and revitalization of the slum areas in large cities.

The government had planned and coordinated a vast assault on poverty. What were the results?

Some programs, such as Project Head Start and job-training programs, were widely praised. Other programs seemed to become stalemated by administration problems or the lack of adequate funding. A few critics said that the war on poverty had been reduced to a "skirmish."

Nonetheless, a large number of people received direct aid. In 1956, 5.8 million Americans received public assistance. In January 1968, four years after Johnson declared "war on poverty," 8.6 million people were collecting welfare payments, and economists estimated that an equal number would be eligible to receive payments if they applied.

In April 1967, Senator Robert F Kennedy of New York and Senator Joseph Clark of Pennsylvania traveled to different parts of the country to observe some of the Great Society programs in action. They found people who were hungry and even starving, as well as children suffering from diseases caused by malnutrition. These unhappy findings were confirmed a year later when the Citizens Board of Inquiry into Hunger and Malnutrition in the United States announced that 10 million Americans were suffering from real hunger. "The situation," warned the report, "is worsening."

During this period of time, the United States had increased its involvement in the controversial war in Vietnam. Military expenditures rose, and Congress cut back spending in nonmilitary areas. The war in Southeast Asia consumed funds and energies that might otherwise have been used for domestic programs.

Despite these difficulties, the country as a whole experienced the longest sustained economic boom in its history throughout the turbulent decade of the 1960s. The GNP—gross national product (the total market value of all goods and services produced in the United States)—doubled.

The decade of the 1970s, however, told another story. Following the withdrawal of American troops from Vietnam in 1972 and a steep climb in the price of imported oil in 1973, the economy faltered. A severe economic recession took hold in 1974 and 1975. The U.S. dollar declined in value, and investments in business decreased. Protectionist moves made by other countries hurt foreign trade. As production in American industry dropped, unemployment rose. Inflation mounted. Life became more difficult not only for the very poor, but for the middle class and for people living on fixed incomes as they struggled to pay escalating costs for food, shelter, and other necessities.

The serious decline in industrial output, the high unemployment figures, and "double digit" inflation were critical issues in the 1980 presidential election. The incumbent, President Jimmy Carter, was soundly defeated by the Republican candidate, former California Governor Ronald Reagan.

During the campaign, Ronald Reagan had asked the American people: "Are you better off now than you were four years ago?" Voters answered with a definite "NO!" as they elected him in 1980. "Government is not the answer to our problem," said the new president in his inaugural address. "Government is the problem."

Reagan's plan for economic recovery was based upon different theories from those that had prevailed during the 1960s and 1970s. The real solution, he maintained, was to reduce government interference and allow the free enterprise system to flourish. Reagan planned on tax cuts that would increase the amounts of money that individuals could save or invest. Lending institutions and banks would then have more money to lend to business and industry. This would, in turn, stimulate the economy, create new jobs, lower inflation and interest rates, and, eventually, "trickle down" to those with lower incomes. More spendable income could also lead to increased consumer buying, which would enhance production and business even more.

The changes in ideology and leadership during the 1980s have had profound economic effects, which will be discussed in the next chapter.

CHAPTER FOUR

# POVERTY TODAY

**I**N its 1986 pastoral letter on the American economy, the National Council of Catholic Bishops stated:

> Harsh poverty plagues our country despite its great wealth. More than 33 million Americans are poor; by any reasonable standard another 20 to 30 million are needy. Poverty is increasing in the United States, not decreasing. For a people who believe in "progress," this should be cause for alarm.

According to statistics gathered by the Census Bureau, the bishops were correct: The poverty rate had increased. From 1973 to 1979, the rate stayed near 11 percent then rose each year until it reached 14.4 percent in 1984. (In other words, it rose by about 33 percent during a four-year period.) Since 1984, it has declined slightly to a rate of about 13.4 percent. What factors might have contributed to this rise during the 1980s?

When the Reagan administration took office in 1980, one of its first priorities was to improve the U.S. economy, which had suffered during the late 1970s. High prices for crude oil and other factors led to high rates of inflation. Although prices were rising, wages remained stagnant, and the purchasing power of the dollar decreased. People who had to spend more of their income on essentials could no longer afford to buy higher-priced items such as new cars or appliances. Money that might otherwise have been spent or invested was used for food and rent. There was a marked decline in the sales of durable goods.

Meanwhile, the high interest rates on loans prevented many businesses from borrowing the money they needed in order to expand or even stay afloat. During the recession that developed in 1981, many businesses had to reduce the number of their employees or shut down. Thousands of middle-class workers suddenly found themselves standing in unemployment lines.

As part of its plan for economic revitalization, Reagan's advisers called for large reductions in government spending. Although the defense and military budgets were left virtually untouched, most other government programs underwent cutbacks.

Federal programs aimed at the poor were especially vulnerable. They suffered budget cuts two-and-a-half times greater than cuts for all other programs combined (about 60 percent of the total budget cuts). Nutrition programs aimed at low-income children were cut 30 percent, and 3 million children were dropped from the school lunch program. The food stamp program, which allows poor persons to buy food staples with stamps provided by the government, was reduced by about 19 percent, and more than 1 million people were no longer eligible to receive the stamps. In *The New American Poverty*, author Michael Harrington points out that the buying power of these benefits had already declined between 1972 and 1981, during which time their real value "fell by 12 percent."

The major cash welfare program for the poor, Aid to Families with Dependent Children (AFDC), was also reduced by about

12 percent. Hundreds of thousands of recipients were termi-
nated from this program, which serves more than 10.3 million
people. Furthermore, Harrington contends that "AFDC benefits, measured in constant dollars, declined by 28 percent
between 1972 and 1981."

In addition, Medicaid funding was cut by $4 billion, and
thousands of people lost their medical coverage. Hundreds of
clinics that had served poor women and children were closed.

Altogether, the income and service supports that benefited
millions of people were greatly reduced and, in some cases, were
completely withdrawn. Unfortunately, these cuts came at a time
when nearly 11 million people were out of work. Fifteen percent
of the population—more than 34 million people—had incomes
below the poverty level.

Government economists, such as Budget Director David
Stockman, were optimistic about the future. They believed that
the poor needed jobs rather than "handouts" and that new jobs
would be generated as the economy improved.

There were others who supported the "supply side eco-
nomics" viewpoint that the Reagan administration favored. In
his best-selling 1981 book *Wealth and Poverty*, George Gilder
discussed the importance of creativity, technological explora-
tion, and economic enterprise in the development of a society's
wealth. He questioned whether some of the nation's welfare
programs were truly helpful or whether they led some of the
recipients to develop a debilitating dependency upon the government's goodwill.

These issues were debated in print as well as in conversations
throughout the nation. The "work ethic" had been a part of the
American value system since colonial days. The question was
raised, as it had been for hundreds of years, whether it was
beneficial, in the long run, to give people money they had not
earned. Did it perhaps reduce the incentive to work or to solve
one's own problems more actively? Gilder addressed this "potential for moral hazards" and stated that welfare programs had a
tendency "to reach beyond their mandate." He asserted that

"...the transfers have imposed a rising burden of taxation on working families which has provoked a spirit of anger and frustration."

Prominent economist Milton Friedman also said that programs to help the poor may actually hurt them. In his book *Capitalism and Freedom* (1962), he argued that, although well intended, certain programs such as public housing and farm price supports, had negative effects that were far different from what their originators had intended.

Charles Murray, author of *In Pursuit: Of Happiness and Good Government* (1988) and *Losing Ground* (1984), also criticized certain social welfare programs. He contended that economic growth, not social programs, was the key to alleviating poverty. He expressed the concern that many people who were able to collect welfare payments had withdrawn from the labor market and were contributing to a rise in "latent poverty" (people who would be poor if they did not get welfare payments).

As the debate continued, the Reagan administration passed new tax legislation that reduced the amount of taxes paid by businesses and by some people with higher incomes. The president, many legislators, and economic advisers such as David Stockman reasoned that if people had more money at their disposal, they would increase consumer spending and invest more money in businesses that would, in turn, create more and better-paying jobs. These new wage earners would spend more, too—thus further strengthening the demand for more goods.

Abetted by a decrease in the price of crude oil, the rate of inflation declined. Interest rates also decreased, encouraging investments and making lower-cost loans available to both businesses and to potential homeowners. As interest rates fell, inflation rates decreased, and investments increased, the stage was set for economic expansion.

Critics of the administration, such as Senator Edward Kennedy of Massachusetts, consumer activist Ralph Nader, and political leader Jesse Jackson, argued that the burden of economic recovery had fallen heavily upon the poor. They questioned the new tax law that reduced the maximum tax rate on high-income earners from 50 percent to 35 percent and certain special tax preferences given to businesses.

These and other critics also complained about the administration's defense budget. Those who opposed certain military expenditures, such as aid to the Nicaraguan rebels (or "contras"), said that these monies should fund domestic programs, especially those that would help the nation's poor. One of the organizations that reproached the administration in this regard was the Women's International League for Peace and Freedom (WILPF), founded in 1915 with Nobel Peace Prize winner and settlement-house founder Jane Addams as its first president. In 1985, the WILPF published its "Women's Budget," which sharply criticized the "Reagan revolution." This alternative budget proposed cutting defense spending in half, alleging that it had grown by $149 billion since 1980. The organization also maintained that President Reagan was emphasizing external threats to national security at the expense of "threats that are corroding our society from within...unemployment, hunger, homelessness, rising illiteracy and infant mortality rates...violent crime" and that a transfer of monies toward "health care, housing and education would go a long way toward solving the budget and economic crises in the U.S."

In response to its critics, the Reagan administration pointed to an economic upsurge that had halted the deep recession of 1981–1982 and resulted in noninflationary growth. This might have been good news for several income groups, but other forces in the economy were also at work.

The lowered tax rate was partially designed to help people deposit and invest more money in order to increase the funds available for business loans. These loans would, in turn, permit businesses to modernize plants, purchase new equipment, improve productivity, and create new jobs. In some cases, however, businesses used the money for "takeovers" or "buyouts" of competing businesses. By 1986, corporate mergers

The 1980s saw an increase in poverty among people such as this young family eating in a city soup kitchen. Forsyth/Monkmeyer Press Photo Service

were taking place at the rate of about twelve per day. These takeovers led many companies to reduce their work force or even shut down. As a result, many workers became unemployed.

Concerned about increasing their profits, some American companies chose to move their factories from the United States to foreign countries where wages were lower and regulations governing working conditions were either less stringent or nonexistent. Clothing, television sets, and automobiles were among the goods now being produced by foreign workers. Competition from foreign labor hurt the American job market.

Foreign countries have presented the United States with competition in other areas as well. After World War II, certain basic industries in the United States, including the automobile, steel, and machine tool industries, tended to share large profits with their stockholders instead of using these funds to replace worn-out equipment and modernize production facilities. When their factories became outmoded or inefficient, they could not generate products at competitive prices. For example, when Japanese and Korean steel manufacturers were able to offer their steel on the world market at prices far below that of the American product, thousands of American steelworkers lost their jobs because their plants were closed.

Competition from foreign automobile manufacturers wounded the American auto industry. Some American factories, which were geared to producing larger cars—the so-called gas-guzzlers—lacked the money necessary to modernize their equipment. Unable to meet a growing demand for small, well-designed, fuel-efficient cars (prompted, in part, by an increase in fuel prices), a number of auto manufacturers closed their plants or reduced their work forces. Thousands of assembly-line workers lost their jobs, especially in hard-hit Detroit. There, by 1982, one out of every two citizens was living below the poverty line.

The clothing and textile industries, which have provided manufacturing jobs, particularly in the south, have suffered, too. Since 1982, about 350,000 textile workers have lost their jobs. In 1984, North and South Carolina, where a number of textile mills are located, reported the lowest number of workers in this industry since the 1940s. Even if the textile mills can modernize their plants in order to compete more effectively, fewer unskilled workers will be needed as their jobs become automated—a situation that may intensify.

Those factories that did survive and even thrive frequently

These Japanese cars sitting on a dock at Port Newark in New Jersey testify to the inroads the Japanese have made in the U.S. auto industry, costing thousands of jobs for American workers. AP/Wide World Photos

did so because they had modernized their equipment. As in the case of some of the textile mills, this trend was ominous for a great many workers because automation often led to the loss of their jobs. Robots, directed by computers, are cheaper in the long run than workers. Automated factories can run night and day when demands are heavy, or they can shut down when inventory stocks are too high. Human workers, on the other hand, work a set number of hours every week and expect to be paid during slow periods. In addition, robots and computers don't need pensions, health benefits, paid vacations, or the other "extras" required by workers. From a human viewpoint, though, the cost of automation can be very high.

Another profound change unfolding in the United States during the 1980s was the shift from an economy based on heavy industry to an economy based on high technology and service industries. Rapid developments in electronics and computer technology transformed American society and generated hundreds of new job categories. Jobs in these "high-tech" industries were available to workers who possessed new, sophisticated skills. Workers displaced by factory closings could not compete for those jobs without special training.

The expansion in the "service" economy provided other kinds of job opportunities in such fields of health care services, real estate, retail sales, and restaurants. Many displaced workers sought jobs in the service sector. However, these jobs often offered lower pay and fewer employee benefits than those workers would have received in factory jobs.

According to the government's tally, more than 15 million new jobs have been created during the 1980s. Yet many of them pay less than $10,000 per year. According to the National Commission of Jobs and Small Businesses, more than 1 million manufacturing jobs paying $13 or more per hour were lost between 1980 and 1985, and more than 5.5 million jobs paying $5 to $7 per hour were created in the various service industries.

The Reagan administration noted that in September 1988 the official unemployment rate was lower than it had been for more than a decade. A March 1989 *New York Times* headline declared: "Rate of Jobless in a Sharp Drop to 15-Year Low." The *Times* reported that the nation's unemployment rate had dropped in February 1989 to 5.1 percent and that the 10 percent of the jobless who had been "out of work for more than six months was the lowest in nine years." Both the former president and newly elected President George Bush have contended that the recent low unemployment figures are evidence of a healthy and growing economy.

Other people disagree. They point to statistics that show that many men retired early after they gave up looking for work. In 1970, 10.5 percent of the males between the ages of fifty-five and fifty-nine were retired; today, that number is about 20 percent.

The statistics, say administration critics, don't include these thousands of early "retirees."

Clearly, the economic landscape of the United States has changed substantially during the 1980s. Interest rates and inflation have decreased. High-tech and service jobs have replaced many manufacturing jobs. The tax system has been overhauled, and businesses have received more incentives to encourage growth.

At the same time, goods produced in foreign countries have flooded our marketplace. The trade deficit, a major political issue during the presidential campaign of 1988, has grown so large that the United States now imports more goods than it exports, and spends more on foreign-made goods than it earns from the sale of American-made goods to other countries. "The United States has been transformed from the world's largest creditor into the world's largest debtor," complained Democrats during the 1988 elections. Currently, the United States owes more than $421 billion to foreigners. The annual interest payments alone on this debt are more than $21.5 billion.

Added to these problems is the fact that the government spends more money than it collects in revenues. To meet its expenses, the government borrows money. The debt now stands at an astonishing $2.4 trillion. The national debt was also the subject of much debate during the 1988 elections. Many voters, when polled, identified the state of the economy as the most critical issue facing the nation.

One response to the federal budget deficit was the Gramm-Rudman-Hollings Act, which Congress passed in 1985. It requires Congress to find ways to cut the deficit by a predetermined number of dollars every year. The "deficit target" set for the year 1989 is $100 billion. Thus, the 101st Congress faces difficult choices as it considers such options as spending cuts or an increase in taxes. During the election campaign, candidate George Bush pledged that there would be "no new taxes."

What form will the federal budget take and how will this

affect government programs for the poor? The problem of poverty remains unsolved, and the United States is moving into the 1990s with disturbing images of the homeless, of farm families who have lost their land, of displaced workers, and of 1980s soup kitchens serving food to hungry men, women, and children. There is still unemployment, homelessness, inadequate health care, and hunger.

How widespread is hunger in a nation with extensive agricultural resources? In 1985, the Physicians' Task Force on Hunger in America (PTFHA) released a report that said, "Hunger is a problem of epidemic proportions across the nation." The PTFHA, composed of twenty-two physicians and public health experts from across the nation, was a study group sponsored by the Harvard School of Public Health to survey the problem of hunger in the United States. The report, based upon interviews, home visits, and field studies around the country, stated that 20 million Americans, including about 500,000 children, were going hungry on a regular basis and were suffering from malnutrition.

The report further challenged Congress to respond to the problem, saying, "Today, our leaders have permitted poverty in this nation to reach record levels and then cut back on programs which help our citizens endure economic hardship. As a result, America has become a 'soup kitchen society,' a spectre unmatched since the Great Depression." As evidence, the report cited the increase in the number of soup kitchens and emergency food programs in the United States. (Such programs continue to increase in number. For example, in New York City, there were 30 soup kitchens in 1980; by 1987, there were at least 560.

The problem of hunger, which will be discussed again in later chapters, is only one of the problems experienced by the poor throughout history. We have also examined some of the complex factors in the national and world economies that contribute to poverty. We have also looked at the various ways that government and private citizens have responded to the needs of the poor since colonial times—through the early years of the nation, the Industrial Revolution, the Great Depression, and the decades leading into the 1990s.

Next, we will look more closely at the ways in which poverty affects different people. What special problems and needs arise when resources are not adequate? What can be done to help people to achieve more opportunities for healthy and fulfilling lives?

# CHAPTER FIVE

# THE CHRONIC

# POOR

**T**HROUGHOUT much of the twentieth century, certain segments of the population have remained trapped in a stubborn poverty. Labeled the "chronic poor," these people are found in urban black ghettos, in rural sharecroppers' shacks, among the hills of Appalachia, on American Indian reservations, in migrant labor camps, and many other places not often seen by average Americans.

Many middle-class Americans point with pride to their immigrant parents and grandparents who worked hard and eventually rose up the economic ladder. "All it takes is hard work to succeed in America," they say.

Hard work alone, however, does not guarantee success. In a 1985 study, authors Sar A. Levitan and Isaac Shapiro concluded that:

2 million adults—50% more than in 1978—worked full time throughout the year, yet they and their families remained in

poverty. Another 7.1 million poor worked either in full-time jobs for part of the year or in part-time jobs...[yet] continued to have low earnings. The vast majority who did not work were children, the disabled or elderly persons who can do little to enhance their income.

What, then, are the factors in the lives of these people, many of whom work very hard, that prevent them from enjoying more economic advantages? A look at the lives of some of the "chronic poor" may help us understand these factors.

# MIGRANT WORKERS

No one is certain how many migrant workers there are, but the U.S. Department of Agriculture states that there may be more than 1 million. The Migrant Legal Action Program believes there are more—about 3 to 5 million. (Both of these sources admit that it is difficult to get acccurate numbers, especially of the children and undocumented workers.) About one-third are white, one-third are Hispanic, and the remaining third are black, Oriental, and native American. Because migrant workers move from place to place, anti-poverty programs may have little sustained impact on their lives. Their children often suffer from malnutrition, hunger, lack of education, and the stigma of being migrants.

What is it like to be a migrant agricultural worker? As a child, you would travel from place to place with your parents, your brothers, and your sisters, "following the crops." You would work in the hot sun, picking ripe fruits and vegetables that eventually appear in the stores as fresh produce or canned goods.

You might spend the winter in Florida, picking beans and living in a two-room shack without running water, bathrooms, or electricity. You would have to get water from an outdoor faucet shared with other families, and your "bathroom" would be a drafty outhouse. Perhaps you would live in a run-down trailer or in public housing, such as Farmworker Village in

In a migrant worker camp in Florida, a woman comforts her child outside the trailer where she lives. UPI/Bettmann Newsphotos

Immokalee, Florida. The better public housing projects such as this one, however, have long waiting lists.

Imagine life without even a small kitchen. Your family could not prepare its own meals and would have to eat more pre-packaged foods or buy the food sold in the migrant camps. You would not be able to reach into the refrigerator for a cold drink or after-school snack.

By May, the bean crop would probably be harvested, so your family would load its belongings into the car and head north to New Jersey in order to pick strawberries and onions all summer. Perhaps here, you could live in a cabin with electricity and watch the television in the "community house."

If the weather was favorable, if there was no drought, if the crops were abundant, if no one got sick, if the car didn't break down—and a long list of other "ifs"—your family could then return to Florida with just enough money to pay for necessities until the next harvest.

Wages and working conditions for migrant workers have been slow to improve. During the 1960s and 1970s, farm workers in California, led by Cesar Chavez, formed the United Farm Workers Union. Their strikes against the growers met with strong resistance, but the farm workers eventually convinced some growers to provide better working conditions—portable toilets and handwashing facilities, for example—and higher pay. The actions of the union also resulted in the formation of the Agricultural Relations Board, which helps protect the rights of workers in California.

Despite these gains, only about 5 percent of America's agricultural workers belong to a union. Many migrants don't join because they fear reprisals by growers; they have heard about union members who were fired, beaten, or unable to get work.

Although the workers are entitled by law to receive the minimum wage, currently $3.35 per hour, many work for less. Consider a group of workers picking cucumbers in North Carolina. Their day begins at 7 A.M., and they move along their assigned rows, filling their buckets under the hot sun. A full bucket is heavy—more than fifteen pounds—and the worker must carry it to a truck, where he or she receives a ticket worth about thirty cents. An experienced, robust male worker might pick up to 90 buckets during a nine-hour day, earning $27 for this exhausting work. Meals sold in this camp cost at least $2.50, so three meals would require $8 or more from the day's wages. Rent for poor-quality housing can cost $60 or more per month or even $1 extra per day for each family member.

Another problem is that workers usually lack health insurance, and such illnesses as diarrhea, intestinal parasites, and even tuberculosis are prevalent. Accidents are widespread, too. In the orchards, workers can fall from the tall ladders they must climb to pick apples or oranges. Farm machines pose another hazard. In the fields, workers are exposed to powerful pesticides that are sprayed and dusted on the crops. Workers frequently develop skin infections from pesticides and from insect bites.

In addition, some of the crew leaders ("bosses") and growers ignore laws regarding wages and working conditions. Often, the workers—Hispanics, Haitians, Jamaicans—do not speak English or know about their legal rights. Besides, they may need to earn even a few dollars too desperately to challenge the bosses.

What has been done to help agricultural workers with these and other problems? In January 1983, the Migrant and Seasonal Agricultural Worker Protection Act (AWPA) was enacted to protect the workers from employment abuses. The Migrant Legal Action Program (MLAP) a Washington-based private organization supported by U.S. government funds, is an advocacy group that provides information and legal services to farm workers. In the past several years, attorneys working for this group have brought litigation under the AWPA and also under the Fair Labor Standards Act. The MLAP helps workers negotiate in such pertinent areas as housing, field sanitation, education, and income transfer programs (for example, social security, food stamps, and unemployment insurance).

The Farmworker Justice Fund, a private organization, also provides legal aid to agricultural workers. It has documented cases in which farm workers were illegally brought into the United States and sold into slavery-like conditions, ill fed and ill housed in camps resembling the worst prisons. The workers were so underpaid that they could hardly hope to buy their "freedom." Such cases of "peonage" also have been identified by the Migrant Legal Action Program.

The United Migrant Association, located in Florida, was founded by Benito Lopez and has more than 6,000 members. A migrant himself, Lopez understood the need to publicize the problems of agricultural workers. This association also gives legal assistance to migrant workers.

Efforts have been made to promote communication among the different parties involved with agriculture. The American

Friends Service Committee (AFSC), a Quaker-sponsored organization founded in 1917 to give postwar relief as well as to respond to problems of poverty in the United States, has developed programs in which there are three-way negotiations among farmers, farm workers, and major produce buyers, such as Campbell's Corporation. In 1986, through the Farmworker Labor Organizing Committee (FLOC), the concerns of these different parties were addressed. An agreement with Campbell's that year improved the workers' conditions in such areas as housing, wages, child labor, and exposure to pesticides and also gave protection to the farmers by stabilizing prices and aiding access to processor plants. The contracts set terms for growing and harvesting before planting and also established a sales price.

Because information can help agricultural workers to improve their lives, the AFSC Farm Labor Program also sponsored a radio telecast in 1987 in California's San Joaquin Valley. Speaking in Spanish, host Pablo Espinoza has interviewed teachers, doctors, union members, and labor contractors, providing educational information and answering listeners' questions on the air.

Legal aid, information, education—often, these are keys to alleviating poverty. How difficult is it for migrant children to get a good education? A 1988 ethnographic study (that is, a study in which the researchers lived and worked among migrant families while they gathered information) showed that the migrant lifestyle "produces many barriers to academic achievement and social confidence." The researchers identified problems such as the following: early departures and late arrivals in school, constant and painful goodbyes to friends, social isolation, changing curricula, lack of self-esteem, and the need to contribute to the family income by working in the fields. Added to these problems are a lack of favorable conditions for studying at home and, in many cases, a language barrier.

Understandably, the school drop-out rate among migrant children is high. The U.S. Department of Health and Human Services found that about 60 percent of migrant children quit school before the ninth grade and only about 11 percent enter the twelfth grade.

In many families, the children begin working in the fields for at least part of the day when they reach the age of four or five. Many migrants now realize the advantages of a high school diploma and do not let their children work during school days except when the family has emergency expenses, such as those due to illness. Each time the family moves to a new location, the parents must enroll the children in another school. Because of interruptions in their schooling, the children may lag one or two grades behind their age level. They may dislike school if they feel unable to achieve or when nonmigrant children call them such names as "onion picker." As teenagers, they may decide to quit school and work full time to improve the family's income and to buy such things as nice clothing and record players— things many other teenagers take for granted.

For those migrant youth who do quit school, the Migrant Dropout Reconnection Program offers an alternative way to get an education. It connects potential students to "GRASP"— Giving Rural Adults a Study Program—and is free for those who qualify. Funded by both federal and state monies, GRASP enables students to earn a high school diploma through home study—an advantage if students have had negative experiences in school or lack a means of transportation.

In recent years, the federally funded Migrant Education Fund has provided a wide range of services, including an interstate coordination program that embraces the Migrant Student Transfer System. Originally, the bill provided for children ages five to seventeen; the 1988 version of the bill expanded the coverage to ages three to twenty-one. Services have included tutoring, bilingual literacy, and a drop-out prevention program.

What impact have Migrant Education Fund programs had on the lives of the workers? In a 1988 issue of *MEMO* (the Migrant Education Monthly magazine), a migrant parent was quoted as saying: "For me, it is not just a program. It is something greater....[It] gives a lot of protection to the children....It gave a lot of protection in the schools, a lot with the insurance, the meals in the schools and various programs."

If a program is to have optimum results, people must know enough about it to use it effectively. In the same issue of *MEMO,* another migrant couple complained that although they were told to register in the education program, no one explained it to them: "They didn't say anything about special classes or tutoring or anything like that...."

Another complaint is that some programs don't start early enough or have enough openings for all the children who need them. For preschool children, there are day-care centers in several states, such as Texas and Florida, and there are Head Start programs that serve many infants, toddlers, and pre-schoolers. Funds for these were made available in 1964 when Congress passed the Head Start legislation. Unfortunately, there are long waiting lists at many centers. In Florida, for example, several hundred children wait for vacancies at a center that can take care of 100. Centers rely on funds from the Department of Health and Human Services, and increased funds are needed in order to start new centers or enlarge and staff those that already exist.

Before federal funding became available, various churches— Catholic, Mennonite, and Baptist, among others—had set up and operated day-care centers for migrant children. Churches still operate many of the day-care centers, which give working parents an alternative to taking their very small children out into the hot sun among such health hazards as pesticides and farm machines.

Improving the health of the children is a major focus of the preschool programs. Centers usually serve nutritious meals and stress health education, with some health care being delivered by professionals who live in the community.

Health care for migrants of all ages is provided in some areas by mobile health clinics, and health education is emphasized by migrant organizations. Still, health care remains a major problem, as is clear from these statistics: A migrant worker has a life expectancy of only fifty years, compared to about seventy-four years for the average American, and the infant mortality rate for migrants is more than twice the national average.

Programs offered by private organizations and by the government have helped many people, but the waiting lists—for preschool programs, for educational programs, for improved public housing—show that more help is being sought in fundamental areas. A great deal will depend upon what kind of funding is provided by government, both federal, state, and local, and by the donations and volunteer efforts of other citizens, as well as upon the continuing efforts of the migrants themselves.

## NATIVE AMERICANS

Statistics about poverty among native Americans tell a grim story. The U.S. Bureau of the Census cites the average unemployment rate of native Americans at a staggering 44.5 percent. For the Sioux of South Dakota, the figure reaches 64 percent. Among the Shoshone and Arapaho tribes of Wyoming, 65 percent of workers over age sixteen are unemployed. (These figures are based upon the numbers of Indians who are actively seeking work but have been unable to find it.)

Because of these high unemployment figures, many native Americans have no income whatsoever, and more than 50 percent have incomes well below the official poverty level. More than half of the total population (more than 1.5 million) live on or adjacent to reservations. About 21 percent of their homes have no indoor plumbing, and 16 percent have no electricity. Many native Americans experience the same problems as those that afflict migrant workers and others—malnutrition, hunger, and sickness. Indeed, one in every three Indians will die before the age of forty-five, and the life expectancy is about twenty years less than that of the general population.

Ironically, native Americans are among the poorest citizens in a land they once dominated. Since colonial days, white settlers steadily expanded their control of the area that is now the United States, adopting different (and sometimes contradictory) policies toward the native Americans they were displacing. Treaties were often violated as white settlers and the U.S. government appropriated larger tracts of valuable, more productive land and relocated native Americans to "reservations" on less desirable tracts.

Contemporary writers such as Dee Brown, author of *Bury My Heart at Wounded Knee,* have criticized the government's policy of "forced assimilation." This notion, which prevailed from the late 1880s to the 1930s, held that the Indians would become truly civilized by adopting the white man's customs, appearance, and religion. Indian children were coerced into attending white schools or even boarding schools, and parents risked the loss of valuable food rations from the Bureau of Indian Affairs if they resisted such efforts.

Important legislation after 1900 signaled an effort to improve conditions for native Americans. In 1924, Congress passed a law granting them full citizenship. The Indian Reorganization Act of 1934 acknowledged that Indians on reservations had the right to self-government and were entitled to maintain their own cultures. In 1970, President Richard Nixon said that native Americans could be "independent of federal control" without losing aid and support services from the government.

Disruptive events—the loss of native lands and traditional means of livelihood, with the resulting displacement that sent many Indians to cities as refugees, and the efforts to alter the Indians' own culture—are frequently blamed for the widespread poverty of native Americans today. Related problems, such as poor health, malnutrition, unemployment, inadequate education, and illiteracy, have further hindered their economic progress. A health worker visiting an Indian home in New Mexico described the situation of the family she met:

> The father was employed temporarily at odd jobs near the reservation, but had not been able to find permanent employment. The family's food supply consisted of white flour, sugar,

some coffee, and canned soup. Mrs. W. had planted a vegetable garden, but it grew poorly in the desert soil. For dinner, they would have the same meal they had eaten all week: beans, corn tortillas, and perhaps a rabbit if the husband had luck while hunting. No fresh fruits or vegetables. A well, built years ago by the public health service, provides water for the area, but pesticides from nearby ranches have polluted the well. The couple's four-month-old baby has suffered from recurring diarrhea, because the mother was using well water to mix her infant formula before she knew the water was bad. Two years ago, the couple's first child died at age two from a respiratory disease.

What has been done to alleviate some of these problems? Since the 1960s, native Americans, like black Americans have fought for their civil rights. Indians now have more rights guaranteed by treaties, such as the right to a dual citizenship— citizenship of the United States and of their own Indian tribe or native Alaskan village.

In the critical area of health, the government's Indian Health Service provides some essential services. Like many other programs, though, it was affected by federal budget cuts during the 1980s. On the Cheyenne reservation in South Dakota, for example, there is only one physician per 1,480 people, and other health facilities are not adequately staffed. "The health conditions on the reservations are so poor they don't even begin to come up to the level of the average person in this country," said Charon Asetoyer, director of an AFSC Indian Health Education Program in South Dakota in 1986. In an *American Friends Service Committee Bulletin* interview, Ms. Asetoyer stated:

> Our infant mortality rate is eleven percent greater than among all other U.S. populations. Seventy-two percent of the people over forty have diabetes. It is not uncommon to find young people in their twenties with high blood pressure. One child out of every 100 suffers from fetal alcohol syndrome.

Fetal alcohol syndrome (FAS), a result of too much alcohol consumption during pregnancy, can lead to lifelong physical and mental damage, premature birth, and a below-normal birth weight. It is a problem on many reservations. The High Plains Indians have the highest rate of FAS in the world. FAS is preventable, however, and Indian women are being educated about the dangers of consuming alcoholic beverages while pregnant. A program directed by Judy Fairbanks of the group "Women of All Red Nations" was bringing important health information to reservations along the Missouri River. In a 1987 *American Friends Service Committee Bulletin* interview, Fairbanks said:

> We've found that what is most successful in treating alcoholism on the reservation is bringing people back to their Indian traditions.... We try to reinforce the messages people received when they were young...from their elders...to look at themselves and the world with respect and harmony.

The education programs have been striving to reduce alcohol problems among all Indians, as well as pregnant women.

Some critics contend that Indian programs suffered during the 1980s. The Friends Committee on National Legislation, a Washington-based citizens' lobby group, stated in its 1988 *FCNL Newsletter:*

> ...during the Reagan administration no specific proposals were issued by the President's Commission on Indian Reservation Economies. Two bills to continue funding for Indian health services and tribal colleges, as well as six other pieces of Indian affairs legislation, were vetoed, and funding for Indian housing and sanitation facilities was reduced, without being replaced by new legislation.

As the 101st Congress convened in early 1989, a number of committees, especially the Senate Select Committee on Indian Affairs and the House Interior Committee, were ready to address issues of vital importance to native Americans. Since spring of 1988, the Special Committee on Investigations has been examining charges of fraud and corruption on the part of federal agencies that administer certain Indian programs. In the February 1989 *FCNL Newsletter,* Chairman Senator Dennis

DeConcini of Arizona was quoted as follows: "Many of the Indian programs are fraught with corruption...most of the others are marred by mismanagement and incompetence....The abuses are contributing directly to the impoverishment of one of the nation's poorest minority groups."

The committee's hearings will be conducted in two parts. The first will deal with legal issues, crime, child sexual abuse, and the environment; the second will address Indian health and education, housing problems, and natural resource management. Improvements in these areas could enhance the lives of many native Americans.

Aside from programs developed by the government and by privately funded organizations, native Americans have worked hard to help themselves. Some tribes have reduced unemployment by creating businesses, such as fisheries, that brought more prosperity to their tribes. They have also worked to improve their schools and have developed special schools that teach children about their Indian heritage, as well as the skills and knowledge they need to succeed outside the reservation.

The federal Office of Indian Education grants money to these tribal schools and to local educational agencies. It also works to promote adult education and literacy.

Housing, adequate nutrition, health care, education, jobs, and safe water—these remain fundamental and painful problems for native Americans as our nation moves into the 1990s.

## THE POOR OF APPALACHIA

Hard times are all too familiar to many residents of Appalachia, that region among the Appalachian Mountains that stretches from Pennsylvania to northern Alabama. In the days when work was more plentiful than it is now, it was often work in the lumber business, steel mills, or the coal mines—difficult, poorly paid, and dangerous. Those men that labored in the "deep mines" often got black lung disease, called miner's lung, and cancers and emphysema are much more common here than in the general population.

Once, much of the economy in Appalachia depended upon coal mining. The use of coal has declined throughout the twentieth century, and new machines to mine coal further reduced manpower requirements. The area's income from coal diminished sharply.

In addition, a number of floods have damaged the land, compounding the area's transportation problems. The winding mountain roads, often described as "treacherous," are frequently narrow and pose dangers for trucks carrying heavy loads; thus, businesses may be reluctant to establish themselves in those areas where they will have difficulty moving materials and products in and out.

Appalachia has been the focus of increased government attention since President Kennedy visited the region during the 1960 campaign. Kennedy saw thin, hungry children, run-down shacks with tin roofs, and people who lived without jobs, health care, or indoor plumbing or running water. The lack of industry and jobs had left many communities without the tax base they needed to pay for services for their citizens or to attract new industry.

As president, Kennedy supported the Area Redevelopment Administration, established by the Department of Commerce in 1961, and the Appalachian Regional Commission, both of which were designed to improve the economy in the region. Private industries were given tax incentives to establish plants in Appalachia. With increased employment, people could support themselves and also pay taxes to revitalize other parts of their communities.

Efforts were made by the people themselves to improve their local economies. In his 1964 book, *War on Poverty,* then Vice President Hubert Humphrey (who had been a senator from Minnesota) described community efforts in a town called Hazleton, Pennsylvania:

In 1956, the mines were flooded by Hurricane Diana. This was the death blow to a community that had been collapsing for thirty years. Overnight, half the work force was unemployed. ...The people...rolled up their sleeves and went to work. With help from the federal government, they formed a local company called CANDO [Community Area New Development Organization]. They raised over 2 million dollars from the local utility companies, banks, and stores...[and] planned an industrial park. They brought fifteen new industries into town. They created 4,000 new jobs. Unemployment is down from 50 percent to 8.5 percent.

However, many communities could not make the kind of progress that Hazleton had achieved with its CANDO program, and poverty in Appalachia was still a serious problem when Lyndon Johnson became president in 1963. Consequently, several Great Society programs focused on this region. One of them was a public works program for the eleven states in Appalachia. Nationwide programs, such as VISTA (Volunteers in Service to America) and Head Start, were also expected to help Appalachia.

Yet as we discussed in Chapter 3, the "war on poverty" did not solve the problem of poverty in America, especially in such "hard core" disadvantaged areas as Appalachia. There is still hunger, inadequate housing, unemployment, and poor health care. About 30 percent of the area's families live below the poverty line and many depend upon welfare payments, sometimes for periods of six years or more.

A forty-five-year-old Kentucky woman, who had testified in Washington before the Select Committee on Hunger, described conditions in her rural community:

I see a lot of hunger, even with the food stamps. They don't buy enough. The price of food and everything keeps going up. Most of the men, they can't find work. I don't care for welfare myself, but some people say, well, a job can come and go, you can't count on it. But the welfare check always comes.

What can be done about conditions such as these? Job

A six-year-old girl in Mud Creek, Kentucky, watches her mother prepare the family's first meal of the day—a watered-down can of stew for lunch. UPI/Bettmann Newsphotos

training and employment are two of the answers most frequently given to this question. In his 1982 book *The Underclass*, Ken Auletta describes a program in Appalachia directed by the MDRC (Manpower Demonstration Research Corporation) a nonprofit group that developed a "supported-work program." This program combined "supportive counseling and training and a one-year job" and was offered to long-term welfare recipients and school drop-outs, among others. In the West Virginia MDRC program, there were 1,054 workers enrolled in the program during a five-year period and "almost 400 completed the training program and went on to regular, unsubsidized jobs," says Auletta. The directors of this and other job programs in Appalachia say that in order to be more successful, programs must help the participants with job-interview skills, transportation needs, education, and literacy.

The Save the Children Federation, a private, nonprofit organization, which was founded during the depression in 1932 and now "provides technical and financial assistance" to communities around the world, began its first self-help program in Harlan County, Kentucky. Save the Children works with government groups, other voluntary agencies, and community agencies to define local priorities and locate resources in order "that the multiple causes of poverty are attacked through an integrated plan that may include health and nutrition education, agricultural production, economic self-sufficiency, credit and loan programs, housing and education." In the Kentucky program, in 1932, for example, Save the Children developed a noontime meal that became a model for the first federal hot lunch program developed years later. It has also administered a day-care center nutrition program, funded by the U.S. Department of Agriculture, and it facilitated a business called "Appalachia Fireside Crafts," which was started in 1968 by five women and which now provides supplementary income to families in fourteen counties of Kentucky and Tennessee. A clean drinking water project and community gardening and canning projects also have been carried out in Appalachia to help residents improve their health and quality of life.

The poverty in Appalachia shows how changes in industry and in the national economy can effect a region's livelihood. Many problems remain unsolved as the depressed areas in Appalachia continue to adjust to these changes.

## BLACK AMERICANS

Today, the 29,306,000 black Americans account for 14.3 percent of the U.S. population, making them the nation's largest minority group. Despite the gains achieved since the civil rights movement of the 1960s, blacks still experience a disproportionate share of poverty. Although one out of every eight white persons is poor, nearly one out of every three black persons lives in poverty.

In Chapter 2 we looked at the impact of slavery and its aftermath on the economic conditions of many black Americans. After the Civil War, many remained in agriculture, some as tenant farmers or sharecroppers on the plantations on which they had been slaves. Some moved to cities, where they took low-paying jobs because they had not received the training or education for better-paying jobs. Racial discrimination prevented many blacks from participating in important economic and political activities of society at large.

In 1954, the Supreme Court unanimously ruled that segregation in the public school was unconstitutional. The following year, bus segregation was declared unconstitutional by a federal court. These rulings paved the way for changes in the laws, customs, conditions, and attitudes that had oppressed generations of black Americans.

The Civil Rights Act of 1964 banned discrimination in jobs, voting, public accommodations, housing, and other areas of life. In June 1966, the Voting Rights Act struck down such practices as poll taxes and literacy tests that often prevented blacks from exercising their right to vote. One month later, Congress approved the War on Poverty bill, and the programs funded by this bill were expected to improve the lives of black Americans and others.

Since 1966, many gains have been achieved. More than 6,000 black Americans have been elected to public office, including the mayors of such cities as Atlanta, Los Angeles, Chicago, Detroit, and Philadelphia. Blacks have started businesses and joined the professions in increasing numbers and have become prominent in such fields as education, journalism, and science.

But black poverty is still an enormous problem. In 1970, 7.5 million blacks were living at or below the poverty level. Today, the number is 8.9 million. Nearly 43 percent of black children live in poverty, according to the Census Bureau. The black unemployment rate is two-and-one-half times greater than the unemployment rate for whites. In 1987, 13 out of every 100 black workers were looking for a job, whereas only 5 out of every 100 white workers was seeking work. According to the U.S. Department of Labor Statistics, one out of four black high school graduates under the age of twenty-five is unemployed.

Black incomes are also lower than those of whites. In 1986, the median family income for whites was $30,809 per year, whereas the median family income for blacks was $17,604. In 1986, about 45 percent of black families had yearly incomes of less than $10,000.

Although many poor blacks live in rural areas, black poverty is most heavily concentrated in cities. Along with the usual problems associated with poverty—lack of good education, low-quality housing, poor nutrition and health care, and fewer good job opportunities—residents of many cities must contend with high rates of crime, drug abuse, and gang violence.

In *The Underclass*, Ken Auletta describes a conversation in which citizens of a black urban community in New York City discussed these and other problems. They pointed to the lack of jobs as a major factor in crime and in alcohol and drug abuse. A man named Henry, whose brother had been robbed and stabbed the night before, said, "The community got no jobs. The people have no money. They will rob other people." Another participant, Leon, added, "...we are human beings like everybody else. And we have these needs—for shelter, clothing, food, for good jobs, good-paying jobs." Others in the group criticized the parents who failed to supervise their children properly—"The parents don't have time for them," said Pearl—and the negative influences of people in the community who provide unhealthy role models for young people.

Attempts are being made in different communities to address this latter concern. Chicago, Detroit, Philadelphia, Newark, and New Haven all have "Big Brother" programs initiated by black leaders to match up young blacks with older men who have studied and worked to achieve success.

Jobs and job training, along with preventing high school students from dropping out, are at the center of other programs. The Manpower Demonstration Research Corporation developed a program for young people between the ages of sixteen and nineteen that combined employment opportunities with incentives for staying in high school. In November 1980, the MDRC reported the results of an eighteen-month program, concluding that "Youth entitlement is a strategy with promise." The report stated that the entitlement program led to a 62.5 percent increase in the rate at which former drop-outs went back to school, and that there was a 90 percent increase in the level of youth employment in the demonstration cities (such as Baltimore, Philadelphia, and Detroit) and areas (such as rural southern Mississippi).

Because many disadvantaged youth live in homes headed by a single woman, legislators and others, such as 1988 presidential candidate Governor Michael Dukakis of Massachusetts, have emphasized the need for quality day-care facilities throughout the nation and for expanding the Head Start programs. Child care is often expensive or nonexistent, as will be discussed in the next chapter. The lack of child care can prevent a mother from becoming employed.

Of major concern to black Americans and others across the nation are the need for adequate housing, health care, and employment; quality child care, schooling, and jobs; and community problems of crime, broken families, and substance abuse. During the 1988 presidential primaries, candidate Jesse Jackson focused on these social issues. Speaking to the Democratic Convention, he discussed the need for government and citizens to work together toward social and economic justice and to "keep hope alive."

Like native Americans, blacks have had to endure racist attitudes from the larger society, and they were displaced from their homelands and traditional ways of life. They were denied education during slavery days, and they have suffered more from unemployment and poverty than white Americans during economic slumps. They still experience a disproportionate share of poverty, a problem that must be addressed as the nation enters the 1990s.

# CHAPTER SIX

# WOMEN AND

# CHILDREN

**I**NCREASING numbers of women and children are living in poverty. One disturbing statistic is the increase in the number of poor children. Today, about four out of every ten people living in poverty in the United States is under age eighteen, even though children make up only 27 percent of the total population. Altogether, nearly 14 million children—one out of every five—is poor, according to Bureau of the Census statistics. In some cities, such as New York, one out of every three children is poor, and one out of every two black children is poor. More than half of all poor children live in single-parent families headed by a woman. Two-thirds of the adults living in poverty are women.

Growing up poor involves special problems that may begin even before birth. A poor woman may not be able to pay for adequate health care or a nutritious diet during her pregnancy. (Teenage mothers are particularly at risk in this regard.) A large portion of the human brain develops during the first few months of pregnancy, a time during which some women do not even know they are pregnant, especially if the pregnancy was unplanned. In addition, poor women may be exposed to health hazards in certain low-paying jobs, or they may do physically demanding work that undermines their own health and that of their unborn children. Thus, a poor child may suffer from physical or mental disadvantages or both from the outset.

After birth, poor children suffer in many other ways. Hunger or malnutrition may be a recurring problem. Babies who are not properly fed face numerous risks: stunted growth, bone diseases such as rickets, skin infections, even brain damage or death. There may be no nourishing breakfasts or after-school snacks. A hungry child often lacks the stamina, motivation, or curiosity needed to do well in school.

Another problem is the lack of safe, adequate shelter. Many poor children live in run-down city apartments in neighborhoods infested with drug pushers and other criminals. Some poor children have no home at all and move from place to place with their families, sleeping in public shelters or even outdoors. They don't get to eat or sleep at regular times. They go from one school to another, changing teachers and friends, and their schooling is frequently interrupted.

Being poor means doing without a lot of things that other people take for granted. Parents of poor children cannot afford to buy food, clothing, and health care they need, much less pay for school field trips, movie tickets, or a visit to the zoo.

The parents of poor children may be unemployed factory workers, workers in low-paying jobs, or farmers who have lost their farms. Perhaps the child lives with just one parent, either because the parents were divorced or because they were never married. Changing attitudes about divorce and sexuality have contributed to the rise in the number of single-parent homes. Since 1970, the number of single-parent families has doubled; they now account for 26 percent of all families. As we have seen, more than half of these single parents are women.

A poor single mother discusses her children's medical problems with an employee at a public health clinic. Rhoda Sidney/Monkmeyer Press Photo Service

Why has the burden of poverty fallen so heavily on women and children, and what steps have been taken to help them? To answer this question, it is helpful to look at the position of women and the attitudes toward them in the United States' past. Although women have been an important part of the work force since colonial times, many legal rights were denied to women until well into the twentieth century. For example, it was not until 1920, after a long struggle by the women's suffrage movement that the Nineteenth Amendment granted women the right to vote.

In addition, women were denied the educational, social, and economic opportunities enjoyed by men. Because most people, including many women, believed that "a woman's place is in the home," women seldom pursued careers and were discouraged from doing so. Women who did enter the workplace were limited to low-paying occupations such as teaching, nursing, clerical, and domestic work.

Women who sought jobs in industry were often viewed as temporary workers, limited to jobs that paid less than comparable jobs held by men and denied promotions and advancement to management positions. For instance, during World War II, women flocked to work in factories and defense plants to fill the jobs left vacant by men who had entered military service. Women were employed to build the tanks, airplanes, ships, munitions, and other materials needed for the war effort. When the men returned at the end of the war, however, most women resumed more traditional roles as wives and mothers.

During the 1960s and 1970s, a number of women worked for "women's liberation," demanding economic, educational, political, and social equality with men. It is now illegal to deny anyone access to housing, consumer credit, education, or job opportunities on the basis of sex.

Despite the gains achieved by women during the past twenty years, discriminatory conditions and attitudes persist. Evidence of the inequality experienced by women in the workplace is found in women's paychecks. For every dollar earned by men in 1987, women earned only sixty-four cents.

Although the law forbids employers from discriminating against women, many job categories are still dominated by men. At the same time that the number of women who now hold executive and professional jobs has increased, working women continue to hold the lowest paying jobs in the economy. They make up the bulk of the work force in offices, retail sales, hospital and health services, restaurants, child care, and cleaning and domestic help.

Even in these jobs, women receive lower pay than their male counterparts. The following figures, from the U.S. Department of Labor, compare the average weekly earnings of men and women who do equivalent work in some representative job categories:

| Job Category | Men | Women |
|---|---|---|
| Office clerk | $322 | $258 |
| Waiter, waitresses | 236 | 159 |
| Nursing aides, orderlies | 234 | 199 |
| Secretaries | 369 | 279 |
| Cashiers | 209 | 172 |
| Computer operators | 395 | 278 |

Women who must support their families have an especially difficult task. Nearly 38 percent of the women who head households live in poverty. Among nonwhite women heads of households, the poverty level jumps to more than 70 percent.

Although many needy mothers work full or part time, most of them lack the education, experience, or skills necessary to acquire jobs with adequate salaries. Without the job skills that are becoming increasingly important as society moves to a more technologically oriented economy, these women are unable to qualify for higher paying jobs.

The situation of Brenda M. shows the difficulty of gaining more skills in order to break the cycle of poverty. Brenda lives in a medium-sized city in North Carolina and, although she works full time, she and her young daughter are poor. They weren't always poor. Before her divorce, Brenda and her family lived in an attractive suburban home. When Brenda and her husband Bill were divorced, he agreed to provide child support payments, but he has not sent any money for the past two years. Brenda struggles to take care of her child, but her job as a bank teller doesn't pay much. Computer operators at the bank earn more, and Brenda would like to apply for such a job, but she must first complete a course in computer operations. Brenda cannot afford the tuition or the cost of a babysitter to take care of her daughter while she attends classes in the evenings. Putting food on the table is hard enough.

Although statistics show record numbers of women in the work force, many are employed in low-paying service jobs such as this waitress in a small Pennsylvania restaurant. Strickler/Monkmeyer Press Photo Service

To outsiders, Brenda and her daughter may seem healthy, but they are anemic and overweight because their diet is based largely on starchy foods that are filling and cheap. Her income is low enough to entitle her to benefit from the food stamp program, but Brenda says she is "not about to take charity." Food stamps and welfare are for "really poor people," she thinks. Even though she does not see herself as "really poor," Brenda lies awake nights, praying that nothing bad happens to herself or to her daughter and worrying about the future.

About half of all the marriages in the United States today end in divorce, and more than half of all the divorced mothers are left to support their children alone. The majority of fathers do contribute to the support of their children, but about 40 percent pay nothing. Child support payments are often inadequate. In 1984, the average amount paid for child support amounted to slightly more than $2,000—hardly enough to buy food alone.

During the 1980s, more strict laws were passed in every state giving local officials the right to withhold child support payments from the paychecks of "delinquent fathers" or to seize their assets until payments are made. However, these laws are sometimes difficult to enforce, resulting in situations like that of Brenda and her daughter.

Pam L., another working single parent, lives in Chicago with her daughter, age six, and her son, age three. Pam does not receive any child-support either, and she works full time in the accounting department of a large "chain store." Pam's "take home pay" is $912 a month. With that, she must pay the rent for a small three-room apartment ($340 a month), food ($280 a month), child care (about $200 a month to a neighbor who watches several children), and transportation to and from work, as well as elsewhere in the city ($30 a month). That leaves about $62 for all other expenses: utilities, medical and dental care, clothing, shoes, and other items. There is never enough money to pay for all these expenses. Recently, Pam sold her ten-year-old car because she could not afford the cost of operating it.

Pam finished high school and planned to study nursing, but she became pregnant with her first child. When she and her children's father separated, she worked for a while at an auto dealership, which later went out of business. For almost a year, Pam and the children received AFDC (Aid to Families with

Dependent Children). Pam did not want to continue "on welfare," so she moved to a cheaper apartment in a neighborhood that doesn't have a park or as good a school system as her former neighborhood did and eventually found her present job.

Many other Americans have relied upon AFDC for varying lengths of time. Currently, approximately 11 million people receive AFDC payments. The average national monthly payment is $122.19 per person. Because AFDC payments are regulated by the states, payments differ widely from place to place, with a high of $277.44 per person in Alaska and a low of $38.57 in Mississippi.

Among these AFDC recipients are a growing number of unwed teenagers. The number of out-of-wedlock births is rising and has increased by more than 15 percent since 1982. In 1985, 828,174 children were born out of wedlock. More than 280,000 of these children were born to mothers under the age of nineteen.

The problem of teenage pregnancy persists, despite sex-education classes, family-planning clinics, and numerous other programs. In 1986, nearly 1 million teenagers—more than one in ten girls between the ages of fifteen and nineteen—got pregnant. About half had miscarriages or abortions; the other half gave birth. Of these, more than one-fourth already had at least one other child.

These teenage mothers face many difficulties. If they do not continue their educations or learn job skills, they will be limited to jobs that may pay even less than their AFDC allotments. If they want to work, they will need to find and pay for child care. To enable teenage mothers to finish school, some cities, such as Washington, D.C., have put day-care centers inside both high schools and some junior high schools where there are significant numbers of students with children. The students can then attend school while their children are cared for on the premises; in some cases, they can also spent part of the day, such as lunch time, with their children.

Such programs address a real need because statistics show

that most AFDC recipients are not well educated. Approximately 60 percent did not graduate from high school, and nearly 75 percent are "functionally illiterate." This poses barriers to helping welfare recipients become part of the work force. Remedial education in reading, writing, and arithmetic has been offered as one solution, along with job training and job placement programs.

Affordable day care, mentioned previously, is another hurdle to employment. In some areas, especially low-income and inner city neighborhoods, day-care facilities are limited or nonexistent. In places where day care is available, the cost may be more than many women can afford while working at a low-paying job.

Even when a woman has job skills and affordable child care, moving from welfare to the work force may entail other problems. When a woman stops receiving welfare, she may no longer be eligible for Medicaid payments that pay doctor bills and other health care costs. Paying for private health insurance, if such insurance is not provided by her employer, may deter a woman from taking a job. She also may be unable to pay for transportation to and from work.

For women with very low incomes who rent their housing, two government programs are especially important. Commonly called "Section 8" and "public housing," the programs are administered by the Department of Housing and Urban Development. Section 8 provides people with assistance in paying their rent, and public housing helps to construct low-income rental units. However, these programs have been cut back since 1981. Former Congressman Jack Kemp of New York was appointed by President Bush to head the Department of Housing and Urban Development. When he assumed this post, he stated that meeting the need for low-income housing and providing solutions to the problem of homelessness in the United States would be two of his department's top priorities.

Several bills introduced in the Congress in early 1989 address the various concerns of women, especially poor women with children. Congressman Bruce F. Vento of Minnesota is sponsoring a bill that would provide additional funds for existing permanent rental housing. Single women have made increasing use of rental housing because they often cannot afford to buy a home. Yet the U.S. supply of rental housing has decreased in recent years because of demolition, conversion to cooperative or condominium housing, and an increased demand. The passage of Congressman Bruce F. Vento's bill would help to meet this need.

Several new bills are concerned with the needs of children. A bill sponsored by Congressman Augustus F. Hawkins of California seeks to establish child care programs in schools, as well as in Head Start programs. Hawkins is also cosponsoring (with Congressman Goodling of Pennsylvania) a bill to reauthorize child nutrition programs. Between 1982 and 1987, these programs (including the school breakfast and lunch programs, the summer food program, and the child care food program, which operates in day-care centers) were cut by about 27 percent. This conclusion was reached by the Children's Defense Fund, a nonprofit, nonpartisan public charity that works to educate the nation about the needs of children and to influence policies that will help meet those needs. As we have seen, good nutrition is vitally important for both mothers and children and can often affect lifelong physical and mental development. A national child care program (called the "ABC bill") is being cosponsored in the House by Dale E. Kildee of Michigan and Olympia J. Snowe of Maine.

In addition, the Equal Rights Amendment, which was not ratified in the past, is being reintroduced by Congressman Don Edwards of California along with 132 cosponsors. Some women's groups, such as the National Organization for Women, believe this constitutional amendment will further protect the rights of women in employment and other areas of life.

Without education, job placement, affordable child care, and decent housing and health care, many women and children will remain caught in the "welfare trap." Clearly, many problems must be addressed in order to alleviate poverty among the nation's women and children. The Children's Defense Fund emphasizes the need to strengthen supports for American families—with programs, funding, and priority setting—and points out that children are a "voteless 61 million citizens whose survival and quality of life are the single most important determinants of the quality of our national future."

CHAPTER SEVEN

# THE ELDERLY

**T**HE next twenty-five years promise to bring about social changes as millions of people join the ranks of the elderly. In 1950, people aged sixty-five and older made up about 8 percent of the population. Today's 26 million elderly make up 12 percent of the population. By the year 2020, their ranks will swell to more than 44 million and will account for more than 17 percent of the population. Moreover, people eighty-five and older are currently the fastest growing segment of the population.

Clearly, Americans are living longer and, for some citizens, the years after sixty-five are "the best years of their lives." Healthier, more active, more affluent, and with more leisure time to pursue their special interests than any other group of elderly in history, they show that old age can be a creative and productive time.

The bright image of energetic and happy old age appears

increasingly in the media and may overshadow the haunting image of the elderly poor. Yet the elderly poor are still among us and include substantial numbers of people.

When the war on poverty was launched in the 1960s, nearly one-third of the elderly lived below the poverty line. Since then, cost-of-living adjustments (COLAs) in social security payments, the Medicare insurance program that absorbs many health care costs of the elderly, and other government programs for the aged have helped the nation's senior citizens. However, they have not eliminated the problem of poverty among the aged. Today, more than 15 percent of all people over age sixty-five—nearly 4 million people—live in poverty, and about 25 percent live on or just above the poverty line.

Women and minorities are particularly hard hit. Because many of them did not hold regular jobs throughout their lives or because they held low-paying jobs that did not include pension benefits or give them much chance to save, old age means not just retirement but poverty. Older women's chances of being poor are twice that of older men. Among elderly black people, nearly one-third exist on less than $5,300 per year. Fifty-five percent of elderly black women living alone subsist on that amount or less. This increased poverty among elderly black Americans can impair their health, nutrition, and housing—all the areas of life affected by economic deprivation.

Elderly Hispanics, who make up the fastest growing segment of the sixty-five and older population, are not better off. According to a report issued by the National Council of *La Raza* to the House Select Committee on Aging, the nation's nearly 1 million elderly Hispanics have a median per capita income of less than two-thirds that of whites, and their poverty rate is twice as high. One in four elderly Hispanics receives no Social Security benefits, compared to one in twelve whites.

The elderly poor face many problems. Finding adequate, affordable housing is one of the most formidable. Of all persons sixty-five and older, 20 percent live in substandard housing, whereas only 3 percent of the elderly reside in low-cost, government-sponsored Housing and Urban Development program housing. Reduced income, health problems, and the desire to live independently while remaining in familiar surroundings often limit the housing options that are open to the elderly poor.

The 55 percent of the elderly poor who live in metropolitan areas face special problems. Confined to urban ghettos and deteriorating neighborhoods, they may face not only substandard housing, declining social services, and rising costs, but also an increasingly violent society. Many old people in cities live in fear of muggings and other crimes. Physically less able to defend themselves, the elderly are frequently the victims of criminals.

Why do the elderly poor remain in unsafe neighborhoods? The most common reason is that they cannot afford to move to better areas. Another reason is that their lives are tied to their neighborhoods by social networks. They may stay in a familiar place, even though it has become run down and dangerous, in order to live among long-time friends, shop in stores where they are known, and participate in churches, synagogues, and other social activities that have been an important part of their lives.

Sometimes, the elderly are forced to move when their apartment buildings are demolished or converted into higher priced cooperative units. If they cannot find other housing or stay with friends or relatives, the elderly may even become homeless—a problem that will be discussed further in the next chapter.

A person who is suddenly displaced in this way confronts vast problems. Some of the "newly poor" elderly do not know how to collect public assistance. They also need a mailing address to which their social security checks can be sent. Alone and confused, an elderly poor person might live out his or her life in hardship and neglect.

Housing also may be a problem for elderly people who live in rural areas. The Housing Assistance Council (HAC), a nonprofit group that works to improve housing for rural low-income people, and the American Association of Retired Persons (AARP), the nation's largest and most politically active organization of the elderly, recently issued a report on the problems of older farm laborers. According to the report, farm workers have an estimated life expectancy of less than fifty years, so their discussion of "older" farm workers covers people forty-five years of age and older. A mixture of blacks, whites, Hispanics, native Americans, and other minorities, these workers face a host of problems, but the shortage of adequate housing is especially acute. As many as one out of every three elderly farm workers lives in a shack without indoor running water. In an effort to improve this situation, the HAC and AARP formed the Older Farmworkers Housing Project, but they have had difficulty finding the funds they need to build more low-cost housing for older farm workers.

As the number of elderly people increases, the housing problem can be expected to grow more severe, but finding adequate housing is only one problem facing the elderly poor.

The cost of health care is another serious problem. The costs of treating a long-term illness can deplete even a lifetime of savings and result in poverty for an elderly person and his or her family.

Medicare, the federal government program that pays part of the medical expenses of citizens over the age of sixty-five, was approved by Congress in 1965. Although the Medicare insurance program has helped thousands of elderly people cope with their health care expenses, it still does not cover all expenses. Medicare is composed of two parts. The first part, which covers hospitalization and acute care, is funded by payroll deductions and employer contributions. The second part, which covers doctors' fees and out-of-hospital expenses, is funded through general revenues and monthly premiums paid by the elderly themselves. Because of rapidly escalating health care costs, monthly Medicare premiums have risen from $9.60 a month in 1980 to $24.80 a month in 1988, an increase of more than 250 percent during the past eight years. Many of the elderly who live on fixed incomes at or near the poverty level simply cannot afford to pay this monthly premium.

Housing can be a severe problem for elderly people in both urban and rural areas. Strickler/Monkmeyer Press Photo Service

In 1980, Medicare payments totaled $50 billion, and by the year 2000, Medicare costs are expected to rise to more than $2.1 billion. Despite these expenditures, seniors are now paying 60 percent of their health care costs out of their own pockets. There have been government cuts in Medicare spending. As part of the plan to reduce the national budget deficit, the administration cut Medicare outlays by $2.1 billion in 1988, and a further cut of $3.8 billion is planned for 1989.

Critics of the current system have argued that, instead of cutting back on Medicare, the government should expand coverage to provide protection for catastrophic illnesses. Rapid advances in medical science during the past few decades have made it possible to prolong life. Heart surgery, organ transplants, kidney dialysis, and other techniques have added years to peoples' lives. However, sophisticated medical treatments and long-term care in hospitals and nursing homes can cost a great deal of money.

The greatest fear of many elderly people is that they will suffer from a prolonged illness that will consume their savings and income and lead themselves and their families into poverty. To help prevent this problem, Congress passed the Medicare Catastrophic Coverage Act, which was signed into law on July 1, 1988. This law takes effect in stages between 1989 and 1993 and will limit the amounts patients must pay out of their own pockets for hospital services and certain physician services covered by Medicare. It will also pay some of the costs of prescription drugs currently being paid by outpatients and will help pay for long-term care at home, as well as in nursing homes and hospitals.

Significantly, the new law eases the financial burden of the spouses of elderly people who require long-term care. Under the old law, if a husband or wife required nursing home care, the couple had to surrender their jointly owned assets before the patient would be eligible for financial assistance. This meant giving up their homes, cars, and other possessions of value. In order to pay huge nursing home bills, some couples felt that their only choice was to have the titles to their home and car put into the well spouse's name and then to end their marriage with a divorce. When the "spousal impoverishment" provision of the law takes effect on September 30, 1989, spouses of nursing home residents will be able to keep $786 in monthly income and

$12,000 or half of the couple's assets, whichever is greater, and still be entitled to financial assistance.

The new law offers other help to the elderly poor. By 1992, Medicare protection will be extended to all enrollees with incomes below the poverty line. These people will not be required to pay Medicare premiums out of their own pockets. This means that when the new law goes into effect, the elderly poor can obtain health care, even though they cannot pay for it. For the poor, this new legislation offers many benefits that were not extended by the previous law.

However, not all of the health care problems of the elderly poor can be resolved by legislation. Often, the elderly poor do not receive the same quality of treatment given to the more affluent. In some cases, elderly people who might benefit from appropriate treatment have been misdiagnosed as "senile," drugged with tranquilizers, and left in nursing homes with little care or supervision. Public attention was drawn to the need for stricter regulations of nursing homes and other facilities for the elderly poor when it was recently discovered that a California nursing home owner had murdered at least seven of the elderly in her care so that she could cash their monthly Social Security checks.

The Social Security Act, passed by Congress in 1935, is the single most important piece of legislation affecting the elderly. The purpose of Social Security is to provide a source of income for retired workers. When a person begins to earn wages, he or she is required by law to have a Social Security number. This number represents the employee's Social Security account. Throughout the worker's lifetime, a percentage of his or her wages are withheld from the worker's paycheck, and this amount, together with a matching amount from the worker's employer, is credited to his or her Social Security account. When the worker retires, he or she is entitled to receive a monthly payment from the Social Security administration. Full benefits are paid to workers who retire at age 65, and reduced benefits are paid to workers who retire at age 62. The amount a person receives depends upon how long he or she worked and the amount of the payments made into the worker's account during his or her work life. Contrary to what many Americans believe, however, Social Security is not like an insurance policy. There is no Social Security "fund" into which payroll deductions are deposited and then withdrawn at a later date. Social Security is funded by taxes paid by the current generation of workers. When Social Security began in the 1930s, there was no existing fund to pay benefits: The benefits were funded by the people working at that time. In May 1987, the average retired worker received a Social Security check of $491.00, and the average disabled worker received $488.

Old people who, for a variety of reasons, do not qualify for Social Security payments may apply for Supplemental Security Income (SSI), a program established by the 1972 Social Security Act amendments and funded by both federal and state governments. In 1987, the maximum federal SSI payment for a person with no other income and living in his or her own household was $340 per month; for a married couple, it was $510.

Although Social Security and Supplemental Security Income are now adjusted to reflect inflationary increases in the cost of living, it is very difficult for the elderly who have no other source of income to survive on these payments alone. If the average person in May 1987 received $491, as was stated above, the total annual income from Social Security alone would have been just $5,892.

A number of legislators and concerned citizens say that the Social Security system is in need of reform. They predict that, if current spending patterns continue, more than one-third of the federal budget will be spent on the elderly in the year 2025. Because only 15 percent of the elderly fit the official definition of "poor," most of this money is being spent on people who have other resources, including some who are "millionaires." Horace Brock, president of Strategic Economic Decisions Inc. in Menlo Park, California, was quoted in *Newsweek* (February 22, 1988) as saying: "There may have been a contract that what you put

One of New York City's elderly poor, this man is eating his Thanksgiving dinner at a soup kitchen. Kopstein/Monkmeyer Press Photo Service

in, you got back, but not six times what you put in." Brock and others have expressed the concern that when the "baby boom" generation—those people born during the period between the end of World War II and the early sixties—reaches retirement age, there may not be enough money to fund their Social Security payments.

Two bills that deal with Social Security were introduced into the House of Representatives early in 1989, and both bills are designed to make the system more independent: Congressman

Edward Roybal of California has sponsored a bill that would establish the Social Security Administration as an independent agency, and Congressman Gerald B. Solomon of New York has introduced a bill that would exclude the receipts and disbursements from the Social Security fund from being used to calculate the federal deficit.

In regard to the large portion of the federal budget that is spent on the elderly, there is still much debate. Each year, the federal government spends eleven times as much for each elderly person as it does for each child, despite the fact that one out of every five children lives in poverty. Former Commerce Secretary Peter Peterson said that what was once a means to provide income security to the elderly has now become a "vast transfer from the needy young to the unneedy aged."

Other people insist that the federal budget need not be balanced by cutting off programs that assist the elderly. Without Social Security, perhaps more than half of the elderly would be poor. Critics of administration spending policies, among them political leader Jesse Jackson, argue that a reduction of the U.S. military budget would result in more funding for social programs.

Meanwhile, senior citizens have become more vocal and politically powerful. They make their voices heard at the polls and through such organizations as the American Association of Retired Persons. Politicians are aware that issues affecting the elderly can influence the outcome of an election, and Social Security reform is often not a popular issue among the elderly and other voters.

Although the nation faces an increasing strain on Social Security and other social programs as the population ages, another group of Americans are faced with more immediate problems. Workers and farmers who have been displaced because of economic changes during the past decade are struggling to take care of themselves and their families. These people, part of a group sometimes called the "new poor," are the subject of the next chapter.

# CHAPTER EIGHT

# THE NEW

# POOR

**D**URING the 1980s, a new group of poor people was generated by the decline of heavy manufacturing, the increasing competition from other countries, a shift to lower paying jobs in service industries, and the dislocations in agriculture. Many of the "new poor" had steady incomes and comfortable homes until they lost their land or their jobs. The descent from middle-class security into poverty has changed the lives of millions of American workers and their families.

Since 1981, more than 12 million industrial "blue-collar" workers have lost their jobs because of layoffs or plant shutdowns. Major manufacturers of steel, automobiles, and textiles have experienced increasing difficulties in competing with foreign imports. Domestic plants were shut down and, in some cases, reopened in other countries where production and labor costs are cheaper. Since 1981, for instance, more than 1,000 textile plants in the United States have ceased production.

The 1980s have also witnessed great shifts in manufacturing. In order to compete effectively against growing competition from foreign manufacturers, some industries have automated their production facilities. Jobs that were once performed by workers can often be done by robots. For example, machine parts for photocopiers, automobile parts, and television parts can be assembled in this way. Unless a company retrains workers for different jobs, extensive automation may lead to unemployment for unskilled workers.

On the other hand, automation may enable a company to stay in business and compete more effectively with foreign manufacturers. Also, workers are needed to make robots and to keep them operating, and, in that sense, automation can create new jobs and save existing jobs if it enables a company to stay in business.

In the short run, however, automation can lead to the loss of a worker's job, just as a plant shutdown can. What happens to a worker displaced by this kind of change in industry? Typically, he looks for another job, but he may not have job skills that are in demand. In addition, in cities where many people were employed at a plant that closed—a steel plant, for example—a great many other people also will be seeking new jobs.

At that point, the worker and his family must survive by collecting unemployment insurance and using whatever savings they may have. Meanwhile, the mortgage or rent must be paid, food must be bought, utility bills come due, the children need shoes and dental care: The family can "tighten its belt," but only so far. Perhaps the unemployed worker or his wife or both of them will find work in the "service sector"—at a fast-food restaurant, for example. If the wages are much lower than the worker's previous salary, other problems can arise. The family may not be able to continue meeting their monthly mortgage payments. Yet how can they sell their home in an area with a depressed economy? If they decide to move elsewhere in search of better employment opportunities, they face the same dilemma: They may not be able to sell their home, except at a loss.

For many families, the down payment they used to buy their home represents their total savings. Being unable to sell this asset or being forced to sell it for a low price are two more devastating results of losing a job in an area troubled by a large plant layoff or shutdown.

Displaced factory workers have sometimes found new, lower paying jobs or moved to other cities in search of work; some have had periods of employment followed by periods of unemployment; some have relied upon public assistance and food distributed by their unions or by charities. These industrial workers are not alone. Hard times have come to rural America as well.

During the past three decades, the demography and employment patterns of the rural United States have changed in many ways. The recession that occurred in 1981–1982 hit rural areas harder than urban centers. Rural areas had higher rates of unemployment and a slower recovery. It is also important to understand that rural poverty does not always mean farm poverty. Many people in rural areas have worked in factories— in the steel, textile, and apparel industries, for example—and have been unemployed as these industries cut back or shut down. The resulting loss of population has further reduced the tax base and resources in many rural communities. Other rural poverty has developed from the loss of family farms.

Farmers have endured many hardships during the past few years, including fluctuations in the prices of grain and other commodities, high interest rates on loans, severe weather conditions in some areas, declining value of farm real estate, rising costs of agricultural production, and a rash of bank failures.

In December 1985, the federal government authorized funding to bring relief to troubled farmers, but for many farmers it was too late. Since 1981, 620,000 productive farmers and their families—20 percent of the farmers in the United States—have had to abandon their work as farmers. Severe drought conditions in 1988 threatened the livelihood of still others. In November 1988, the federal government announced its plans to foreclose on the farm mortgages of an additional 80,000 farmers because they failed to make payments on their loans.

What factors can lead to the loss of a family farm? Changes in economic conditions are a major cause. In the 1970s, grain prices were higher than in the 1980s. Many wheat farmers took advantage of the federal government's farm loan program in order to buy additional land and equipment and to make improvements to their homes and out-buildings. Some had to borrow money for other reasons, such as a bad harvest. When grain prices were good, a farmer could make his loan payments on time, but when the prices fell during the 1980s, the farmer's income declined.

In order to keep a farm operating, the farmer could try to borrow more money, but interest rates had risen in the early 1980s. The cost of borrowing money was high. What other options did farmers have? Some took jobs in town: Often, both husband and wife worked at other jobs and kept the farm going during the rest of the day or night. Some farmers tried to sell expensive equipment in order to raise money for the mortgage and other living expenses, but the market was glutted with used farm equipment. Buyers were scarce or nonexistent. Farmers who could not make their loan payments faced foreclosures. The banks that had lent them money took possession of their farms and sold them at public auctions.

In some cases, farms sold at public auctions were bought by large agricultural corporations, which added them to their own thousands of acres. Family farms became part of large corporate farms, and people whose families had been farmers for generations, living on the same land, had to find new jobs and new ways of life.

The 1980s have been difficult times for other categories of workers besides those in manufacturing and farming. Small business failures have escalated sharply. During 1986 alone, more than 56,000 small businesses closed their doors, and the owners and employees were left to seek other employment. At

When this farm family could not meet its payments to the Farmers Home Administration, they were forced to sell the farm and many of the family's possessions at auction. AP/Wide World Photos

the same time, in large corporations, thousands of jobs, including well-paid "white-collar," middle-management, and executive jobs, were eliminated as a result of mergers and takeovers. When one company takes over another, it is not unusual for the new owner to "streamline" the staff. During the 1980s, mergers have taken place at an unprecedented rate. During 1986 alone, corporate mergers occurred at the rate of about twelve per day, and thousands of people lost their jobs.

As we have seen, the displaced worker often has limited choices. Should he or she stay in the same area and hope that conditions will improve? Many residents of the southwestern states who lost their jobs in the oil industry have remained in their hometowns, but unemployment remains high.

Should the unemployed worker try to sell his or her home and move elsewhere in search of a job? Homes in economically depressed areas may not be easily sold, as was discussed earlier in this chapter. The loss of the major industry in an area can affect the well-being of the entire community. Businesses— everything from grocery stores to barber shops to bowling alleys—lose customers and may even have to close. The population may greatly decline, new businesses will not find it profitable to locate there, and thus the tax base gets lower and lower.

Some displaced workers, often the younger ones, have chosen to learn new and more marketable skills. They have enrolled in vocational training courses, such as those offered at community colleges, or they have been able to get entry-level jobs with companies that offer training courses to their employees. There are also government-sponsored programs aimed at helping displaced workers.

One such program is the Job-Training Partnership Act (JTPA) passed by Congress in 1984, a program that works with private industry to offer retraining and assistance in job placement. The JTPA offers funding to service delivery areas (areas with a population of at least 200,000) where local elected officials work with private industry councils composed of representatives from local industries and businesses. The JTPA conducts training projects, providing retraining and job placement for people who have lost long-held jobs because of plant closings or technological advances. The government predicts that the JTPA will eventually have helped approximately 1 million unemployed workers.

Other important government programs are aimed at helping displaced workers. The Trade Adjustment Assistance program is designed to help workers who have lost their jobs or whose wages and hours have been reduced because of competition by foreign imports. The Federal-State Employment Service refers employable applicants to companies with job openings and assists people in obtainable training they need to become employable.

Today, approximately 9 million displaced industrial workers and farmers whose former incomes placed them in the middle class are working at low-paying jobs. Seven million of them work thirty or more hours a week, and 2 million have full-time jobs, but all of them have incomes below the poverty line of $11,203 for a family of four.

For some of these displaced workers and their families, unemployment or jobs that pay low wages, combined with the scarcity of low-cost housing, has resulted in the tragedy of homelessness. Displaced workers share this plight with a number of elderly poor, as well as with mentally ill people who are not being cared for by families or by institutions and with teenagers and others who live "on the streets."

Homelessness, mentioned in earlier chapters, has been the focus of increased social and political concern during the 1980s. The National Coalition for the Homeless estimates that more than 3 million people across the nation have no place in which to live. Rent increases, building conversions, demolition of old housing for urban renewal and redevelopment, a shortage of new public housing—all these have been described as we looked at different problems facing the poor in the United States. We have also noted that since 1981, the federal budget for low-income housing has been reduced by about 75 percent.

A survey of twenty-six cities conducted in 1987 by the U.S. Conference of Mayors revealed that about one-third of the homeless families at that time were families with young children and that 22 percent of them had full- or part-time jobs. A survey of Atlanta's homeless showed that 40 percent of the men were veterans and that the fastest-growing segment of the homeless population was made up of children under the age of six.

Many of the homeless are congregated in large cities such as Los Angeles, Washington, D.C., and New York, which are already burdened with poverty, drug abuse, crime, and health

Surrounded by his belongings in paper bags, this homeless man takes a nap in New York's Grand Central Station. UPI/Bettmann Newsphotos

care problems, such as AIDS. These cities have not been able to shelter all the homeless. During 1987, New York shelters and welfare hotels housed an average of 28,000 people per day, and the number of soup kitchens in the city rose from 30 in 1980 to 560 in 1987, but thousands of people still remain on the streets, unsheltered and usually hungry.

For several years, Americans have seen television and newspaper images of homeless people sleeping in bus depots, in cardboard boxes and "shanties" reminiscent of the Great Depression days, on sidewalk hot-air grates, or in subway stations. Private and public charities have responded in a variety of ways.

A few cities provide public shelters for the homeless. These shelters offer meals and a place to sleep. In some cases, medical, legal, and social services are also available. Private shelters, such as those run by church groups and other concerned citizens, can be found in many cities. Yet there is not enough space for the people who request assistance, and many of the programs have been called merely "stop gap" measures or costly but ineffective.

Congressman Charles Schumer of New York has introduced a bill into the 101st Congress to address these concerns. If passed, his bill would set up a demonstration program to analyze whether it is more "cost effective" to house needy families in the so-called welfare hotels (which can cost as much as $3,000 per month) or to build permanent housing for such persons.

Another bill sponsored by Congressman Ted Weiss of New York would enable states to use the Aid to Families with Dependent Children "emergency assistance" funds to "purchase, construct, renovate, or rent facilities" that would give emergency shelter to homeless families.

In addition, Congressman Bruce F. Vento of Minnesota has presented two bills regarding the housing problem: One bill would provide more government funds for existing permanent low-income housing programs, and the second would increase the funds available for emergency assistance to the homeless.

Another bill, introduced by Congressman Barney Frank of Massachusetts, would authorize the expenditure of $15 billion over a period of ten years for the renovation or construction of 7.5 million affordable rental housing units. Homeless people would be given priority in renting such housing.

The problem of homelessness will therefore be the subject of much discussion as the 101st Congress convenes. Both houses of Congress also will be considering the federal budget for fiscal year 1989. The administration has proposed cutting the budget appropriations for emergency programs for the homeless (including shelter programs, the Interagency Council on the Homeless, the Supportive Housing Demonstration, temporary emergency food aid, and emergency food relief) by about 34 percent compared to fiscal year 1988. The housing assistance area of the budget (including public and subsidized housing, loan subsidies, rental housing assistance, rental rehabilitation, and FmHA-assisted housing, which is part of the Farmers Home Administration program) would be cut by about 13 percent if the administration's budget is accepted.

The idea of "home" is treasured by most Americans, and there is wide concern about the problem of homelessness, especially as it affects children. Since 1987, individual Americans have contributed several million dollars to charities that help the homeless. One of the most public of these is called "Comic Relief." It was organized by a group of entertainers who produce and participate in a comic variety program telethon, soliciting financial support to aid the homeless. A similar effort called "Farm Aid" has been collecting contributions to help farm families that are in danger of losing their land.

Current legislation and debate centers on the important issues of how to help the homeless most effectively, as well as how to prevent more people from joining their ranks. Many middle-income families are vulnerable to the economic changes and conditions that have caused financial hardships for the displaced workers and farmers described earlier in this chapter. For all the "new poor" discussed in this chapter and for the middle-income families who are at risk, the questions of how to prevent more people from becoming part of the "new poor" and how to help those who do are of major importance.

Expressing his concern about these issues, Sam Beard, chairman of the National Commission of Jobs and Small Business, has stated:

> For the first time in recent history, our children's standard of living may not equal, much less exceed, our own, because manufacturing employment is declining and real wages and

salaries have been falling since 1972. If we continue exporting jobs and importing foreign goods, we threaten the middle class of America.... Our country is unable to sell many of its products at competitive prices on world markets. Too many of our people are unemployed or underemployed. Several of our great industries are in trouble. Even our advantages in technology and agriculture are fading rapidly.

Then Mr. Beard warned: "The outlook for the next generation is troubling."

Other Americans have expresed similar concerns, and if the U.S. economy is indeed so troubled, then poverty in America may increase: a grim prospect.

Problems in one area of the economy have a negative impact on other areas. World and domestic economic conditions may cause unemployment or lower wages. Natural disasters may compound problems, as often happens in the case of agriculture. People without money cannot buy goods or pay rent or buy homes, which leads to the loss of other manufacturing and construction jobs. Without certain basics—food, shelter, health, an adequate education—people are unlikely to achieve their full potential and become highly productive. Without job training and placement and child care, many people cannot move from welfare to jobs. When resources are finite, as is the case with federal, state, and local budgets, hard choices must be made about the most effective and efficient ways to allocate these resources.

Previous chapters have explored some of the solutions offered to these problems. The next chapter will examine several others.

# CHAPTER NINE

# POVERTY—

# CHALLENGES

# FOR THE 1990s

**W**HAT can be done to improve the living conditions of the poorest Americans? What can be done to broaden their scope of opportunities? What can be done to help the poor—especially children, the disabled, and the elderly—who cannot help themselves? Finding solutions to these problems is one of the toughest challenges facing this country in the 1990s.

Past chapters have focused on the history of poverty in the United States since its earliest days and on the variety of factors that contribute to poverty: changes in the national and world economies, geographic and demographic conditions, natural disasters, social and cultural factors (in the form of laws, customs, and attitudes), family structure, and personal factors (the physical and mental endowment and actions of individuals themselves).

Individuals, groups of people, and the government have

responded to the problems faced by needier Americans. Often, there has been wide agreement that poverty should be alleviated. There even has been agreement at different times about how to help the poor through legislation, education, jobs, job training and placement, and providing for basic needs such as food, clothing, health care, and shelter.

Many different opinions have been offered about the best ways to achieve these goals and about the roles of individuals, private charities, and local, state, and federal governments. Until the twentieth century, many efforts to help the poor in the United States took place in the community.

One of the best known of these community efforts was the "settlement house" concept, which developed at the turn of the century during the reform period described in Chapter 2. Jane Addams, the foremost social worker of her time, founded Hull House in Chicago to help that city's poor immigrants. Hull House sponsored classes in English, job skills, crafts, and health care and started children's nurseries and activity clubs for young people. The settlement also built a playground, gave shelter to working girls who were homeless, and urged the city to develop a juvenile court so that youthful offenders would be treated differently from older, more hardened criminals. Settlement houses in other cities, such as New York, had similar programs and invited community members to develop programs and to contribute their time and skills.

Settlement houses can still be found in many American cities and have influenced other community-based programs begun since the early days of this century. "It is natural to feed the hungry and care for the sick," wrote Jane Addams. "It is certainly natural to give pleasure to the young, comfort to the aged, and to minister to the deep-seated craving for social intercourse that all feel."

Individuals and community groups continue to help the poor in the midst through such efforts as the United Way and with fund-raising events and contributions to organizations such as those mentioned in previous chapters.

Yet throughout the twentieth century, the government has taken an increasingly large role in helping the nation's poor. Numerous programs, both state and federal, are designed to help needy individuals and families. The nation's population is large and diverse, and economic conditions depend upon many factors. Among them are domestic considerations and influences from other countries, and those have led to an increasing role of government in dealing with poverty.

## WELFARE REFORM

One of the major government programs—and one of the most often debated—is the welfare program, which costs about $19 billion a year and is funded by federal and state taxes. For more than twenty years, different reforms have been proposed by elected officials, Cabinet members, social scientists, journalists, and others. Debate about the welfare system typically focuses on these questions:

- Who should receive benefits and how should eligibility be determined?

- How should the amounts of benefits be determined? What are the "standards of need"?

- How should the system be administered?

- What roles should federal and state governments play?

- How can families be made more responsible for the support of their children?

- How can those who are able to work be helped to enter the work force rather than depending upon welfare benefits?

In October 1988, after considering a wide range of proposals, Congress passed a welfare reform bill sponsored by Senator Daniel P. Moynihan of New York. Senator Moynihan has actively studied and written about the problems of poverty for more than twenty years. One major provision of the bill calls for tougher action against fathers who fail to pay child support. States will receive more federal funds to locate unwed fathers who do not make their court-ordered monthly support payments, and family court judges will be required to set higher amounts for child support awards. Another important provision of the bill, aimed at preventing family breakups, requires that states now pay benefits to two-parent families. Fathers will no longer have to leave home in order for their wives and children to receive help.

The most significant provision of this $3.3 billion bill, aimed mainly at putting long-term welfare recipients to work, calls for an expanded job-training program. Every state will be required to have at least 20 percent of its eligible welfare recipients enrolled in "workfare," education, or job-training programs by 1995.

Studies of experimental workfare programs during the 1980s showed that most welfare recipients can stop receiving welfare within at least four years without any other special assistance. However, one-fourth of all welfare recipients remain on AFDC lists for more than ten years. The welfare reform legislation aims to get at least some of these people back to work.

The new bill has other provisions affecting women and children. Mothers of children under age three, or those caring for an ill or disabled child or relative, would be exempt from the workfare training program. Mothers who are themselves sick or disabled or who already work more than twenty hours per week also would be exempt. States would be permitted to include mothers of children as young as age one, and they could require the participation of teenage mothers upon the birth of their children.

Many people are optimistic about the welfare reform package, including Robert Reischauer, an economist at the Brookings Institution, who calls it "a step in the right direction."

The Heritage Foundation, a Washington, D.C.–based politically conservative research and policymaking organization, has also urged "tougher enforcement of child support by absent fathers." According to a Heritage Foundation book, *Mandate for Leadership III: Policy Strategies for the 1990s*:

> The current welfare system tends to pour more money to the middle-class "poverty-industry" of service providers than it gives to the poor....Thus the new administration strongly should endorse vouchers, deregulation of welfare services, and similar consumerist policies that would give the poor the power of choice.

## THE MINIMUM WAGE

In 1984, the Bureau of Labor Statistics estimated that about 8 million people were working for wages just at or below the minimum wage and that another 6 million had incomes just above that level. During the 100th Congress, legislation was introduced to amend the Fair Labor Standards Act by increasing the minimum wage from the current $3.35 to $4.65 by the year 1990.

The bill was not passed by the Senate and was never taken up by the House of Representatives. Congressman Augustus F. Hawkins introduced a bill early in 1989 to update the level of the federal minimum wage. Other legislation is expected to appear. Such an increase might benefit some of the "working poor" who were described in earlier chapters.

## EDUCATION AND JOB TRAINING

Getting a job may help a person begin to rise from poverty. Yet in order to apply for and successfully get a job, an applicant needs at least some basic education and skills. Millions of Americans lack those skills. Thirty-six million adults read below the eighth-grade level, and 30 percent of all children currently enrolled in school will probably drop out before graduation. In order to help these people get jobs with adequate wages and also help American workers gain the expertise needed to compete effectively with other nations, the problems of education and job training must be addressed.

The 1988 welfare reform package requires every state to provide job training, adult literacy and remedial education, and job placement programs by the year 1995. Some states, including California, New Jersey, and Massachusetts, have already instituted large-scale welfare-to-work reforms and have spent funds considerably in excess of those required by the new law. To fund its programs, each state will be required to supply one dollar for every fifty cents supplied by the federal government, but some states will have difficulty meeting that obligation. Louisiana, for example, has suffered economic hardships as a result of cutbacks in the oil industry. In a struggle to balance its budget, the Louisiana state government has had to cut back many existing programs. Another problem is that even if the funds for these training programs were available in Louisiana, there may not be enough real jobs in the local economy to employ newly trained workers.

Education, as well as welfare reform, was frequently discussed by the candidates during the 1988 presidential campaign. Problems such as declining scores on achievement tests, illiteracy, and high drop-out rates, especially in poor, inner city schools, have been the subject of great concern. In his campaign speeches, President George Bush declared that he wishes to be known as the "education president." His administration is expected to focus on the growing problem of providing quality education for all children and reducing illiteracy and drop-out rates in addition to expanding opportunities in adult education.

One education organization, the National Association of State Boards of Education (NASBE), is confronting the special educational needs of children of welfare recipients. Says Phyllis Blaustein, executive director of NASBE, "Helping a welfare mother go to work will not assure the long-term sufficiency of her children.... Breaking or avoiding the 'welfare cycle' means

In Washington, D.C., 41-year-old Joyce Ross is a student in a literacy program. Here she practices her reading while her grandsons look on. UPI/Bettmann Newsphotos

assuring that the children now on welfare have the ability to support themselves and their families in the future." Toward this end, NASBE has launched a privately funded, three-year project called "Joining Forces" to link educators with state agencies that serve poor children and their families. The project aims to help poor youngsters enroll in early childhood programs and to remain in school until they graduate.

## THE HOMELESS AND THE HOUSING SHORTAGE

Along with the need for jobs, education, training, and adequate wages, finding decent, affordable housing is a major problem confronting the poor.

With about 350,000 to 3 million homeless people in the United States, the problem becomes much more urgent. The previous chapter explored this issue and described some of the new legislation designed to deal with it.

A report by the Urban Institute offers this gloomy prediction: "It would not be surprising if, by the year 2000, close to a third of all households, and seventy percent of very low-income households, confronted problems of either housing adequacy or housing affordability." If the Institute is correct, many more Americans may become homeless in the future.

Some critics say that existing housing funds are being mismanaged. Writing in *The New Yorker* magazine (January 25, 1988 and February 1, 1988), Jonathan Kozol described how New York City spends housing funds. The city pays owners of "welfare hotels" as much as $18,000 in rent per year for each room occupied by a homeless family, but allows only $240 per month for rent money to a family receiving AFDC payments. In New York City, where rents are quite high, apartments that cost $240 are not available. Waiting lists for apartments in the city's existing low-rent housing projects are long; typically, an applicant must wait eighteen years for an apartment to become available. Kozol and other critics of current policies maintain that the money being spent to house the homeless in temporary shelters could be better used to build decent, permanent, low-rent dwellings for those who need them. Congressman Schumer's new bill, mentioned in the previous chapter, addresses the same concern.

Congressman Joseph Kennedy of Massachusetts has introduced a bill that supports a system called "mutual housing," which has been tried in some European countries. Working with the National Low Income Housing Coalition, Representative Kennedy developed the National Community Housing Partnership Act, which would give an annual $500 million in matching grants to a variety of nonprofit housing programs. The government would supply some money for construction,

Some of the families chosen to buy into the first cooperative apartment building exclusively for the homeless stand in front of their new home on New York's Lower East Side. Previously they and other tenants had lived in decaying hotels and dangerous, crowded shelters. AP/Wide World Photos

and apartments would be rented at below market rates. The rent would be paid to a nonprofit group or tenants' organization to cover maintenance and operating costs.

Some states have devised other solutions to their housing problems. In New Jersey, for example, the state government offers low-interest loans to builders who promise to sell homes to low-income, first-time buyers. In a lease-purchase agreement, the buyers make a small monthly payment. After a few years, the money the buyer has already paid is considered a "down payment" and the buyer can then get a regular mortgage.

What else is being done to help those without homes? In Atlanta, Georgia, former President Jimmy Carter and his wife Roslyn are part of an organization called "Habitat for Humanity." Along with many other volunteers and using funds from private individuals as well as foundation grants, the Carters help to build homes for the homeless.

People in private industry are also participating in these efforts. James Rouse, a successful real estate developer, has been involved with "Jubilee Housing," a group that builds low-income housing and helps people to find jobs. In 1982, Rouse founded The Enterprise Foundation, which has introduced the concept of combining housing assistance with jobs into twenty-seven other cities.

A proposal made by the National Employee Homeownership Program would offer tax incentives to employers willing to help their workers make down payments on homes.

Many of these programs have helped both the homeless and those with low incomes who need more housing alternatives. The effects of proposed legislation and newer programs remains to be seen. Some of the new bills before the 101st Congress suggest that different approaches will be tried as the United States continues to deal with the shortage of low-cost housing.

## HEALTH AND MEDICAL CARE

In 1985, the Physicians' Task Force on Hunger in America released its report stating that 20 million Americans go hungry on a regular basis. The effects of malnutrition can be lifelong for a child whose mother was poorly nourished during pregnancy or for those who do not get the proper nutrients during the critical growing years. The physicians in the task force were concerned about the health problems hunger can cause, as well as the human suffering. They pointed out that preventing hunger is a way of preventing many other health care costs to society.

Besides hunger, the United States faces other health problems. The nation has a higher infant mortality rate than sixteen other industrialized nations. Twenty-eight percent of women who bear children do not receive prenatal care. Thirty-six million working Americans cannot afford to pay for health insurance.

Congress is considering ways for the federal government to improve health care coverage. One of the proposals before the 101st Congress is the "life care" bill that would pay most of the nursing home and home care expenses for the elderly. Another bill would require all employers to provide health insurance for their employees. Congressman John Dingell of Michigan and Congressman Roe of New Jersey have sponsored two different plans for national health insurance.

The Special Supplemental Food Program for Women, Infants, and Children (WIC) has been cut back in recent years, but new legislation might increase its current funding. A number of studies show that the benefits of this program may well outweigh the costs. For example, a 1979 study by the Harvard School of Public Health showed that for every $1 spent on WIC, as much as $3 may be saved in health care costs for the child later in life. In 1978, the Yale School of Medicine found that infant mortality rates for mothers at risk of malnutrition were three times as high among those women who did not receive the WIC benefits.

Because "cost efficiency" is of concern to policymakers, the area of health and nutrition, especially in regard to children, will be worthy of more attention in the coming years. It may offer some hope of preventing illnesses and other conditions that perpetuate the cycle of poverty.

# DRUGS AND ALCOHOL

Among the ugliest features on the landscape of poverty are drug and alcohol abuse. Enormous profits can be made from the sale of illegal drugs, and many people, especially young ones, have been attracted by the money they can make dealing in drugs or by the temporary "escape" from life's problems that drugs seem to offer.

Critics of the "Just Say No" approach to drug use say that many people need other help as well—in the form of drug education, jobs for teenagers, support for families, and effective treatment programs. Schools in all parts of the United States now have drug education programs beginning as early as the elementary grades. In cities such as New York and Washington, D.C., which are plagued with severe drug problems, treatment programs have long waiting lists. Mayor Edward Koch of New York is only one of the many urban mayors who have asked for more federal funds to increase the city's treatment facilities.

Drug abuse is not just the problem of the poor; it affects all areas of the country. Crime, disintegration within families, infants born already addicted, AIDS—the abuse of drugs brings with it a host of other serious and life-threatening problems.

President Bush has vehemently stated that there is a need for increased effort to fight the scourge of drug abuse. He has appointed former Secretary of Education William Bennett to reorganize and strengthen the "war against drugs." One preventative measure the administration will be considering is that of keeping drugs out of the United States by employing more drug enforcement agents, by using economic sanctions against countries that permit illegal drugs to be grown and shipped to the United States, and even by destroying fields of drug crops with pesticides.

These efforts to limit the "supply" of drugs will be combined with continuing efforts to reduce the "demand" by educating people about the many dangers of drug abuse.

The problem of alcohol abuse, which involves a legal substance, is also serious, especially for people who are experiencing stress in several areas of their lives. Studies by the National Institute of Mental Health have shown that the rates of alcohol abuse and abuse among family members increase when the rate of joblessness increases. The Federal Bureau of Prisons has pointed to an increase in the prison population at times when unemployment rises, and many of the crimes committed involve the use of either drugs, alcohol, or both.

There are different kinds of treatment programs for those who are already addicted to drugs or alcohol. Some of these are sponsored by the federal government through community health centers. There are methadone maintenance programs for heroin addicts, but in cities like New York people are on waiting lists to get this and other kinds of treatment. The well-known Alcoholics Anonymous' self-help program has often served as a model for both drug and alcohol rehabilitation programs. There are also different types of private treatment facilities, but in-patient or out-patient care in these centers may cost thousands of dollars.

The problems of alcohol and drug abuse have negative repercussions for the whole society. They will require a committed effort and new, creative approaches if the United States hopes to enter the twenty-first century with citizens who can reach their full mental and physical potentials.

## JOBS FOR YOUNG PEOPLE

A discussion of poverty in the United States returns again and again to the subject of jobs. Young people, especially minority young people, make up a segment of the unemployed. Various programs now help unemployed youth to train for and obtain jobs, and some new programs have recently been proposed by Congress.

Senator Sam Nunn of Georgia has introduced a bill that would involve young people in different kinds of "national service." This service might involve working as a literacy tutor, working with the homeless, teaching, taking "Meals on Wheels" to the elderly and disabled, providing child care services, or perhaps repairing parts of the nation's infrastructure. In return, participants would get vouchers to pay for college expenses or the down payment on a home.

Senator Barbara Mikulski of Maryland is also sponsoring a national service bill, which would enable the participants to perform their chosen service on weekends for a given number of years.

In discussing these national service bills, some congressmen have suggested that the federal government should end student grants for higher education, replacing that system with the new voucher system. If one of the national service bills is accepted in some form, the benefits to needy citizens and to students seeking financial aid might be significant.

## RESOURCES AND THEIR DISTRIBUTION

The United States, like other nations, faces many decisions about the distribution of its resources. In this country, about 15 percent of the gross domestic product is used to fund social programs. Many other countries spend more on their social programs. For instance, the Scandinavian countries spend about 40 to 60 percent of their domestic product to fund social programs. Holland and Belgium are two of the other countries that spend a larger proportion of their national wealth on social welfare than does the United States.

Some government programs—food stamps, Aid to Families with Dependent Children, Project Head Start, women and child nutrition programs, Medicare—assist the poor. Many other programs benefit large corporations and people who are far from poor. These programs include mortgage interest tax deductions, price supports, tax incentives for businesses, and low-interest government loans, among others.

How should resources be allocated? What programs should be funded and where should the money come from? These are central questions that arise in discussions about programs for health, education, and welfare.

Some members of Congress and others suggest that money to fund anti-poverty programs could be raised by cutting off some of the tax "loopholes" that benefit large corporations. There have been years during the 1970s and 1980s when large profitable corporations such as General Dynamics and Boeing Corporation have paid no income taxes.

The American Catholic Bishops' pastoral letter, mentioned previously, suggested that the military budget should be reduced in order to increase funding for anti-poverty efforts. Other groups—the Women's International League for Peace and Freedom, the Friends Committee on National Legislation, the American Friends Service Committee, and others, as well as many American citizens, support this idea.

Would Americans be willing to pay more taxes in order to help its needier citizens? Great Britain, West Germany, Sweden, and Italy are some of the countries where tax rates are higher than in the United States. One poll taken during the 1988 election found that a majority of those polled said they would be willing to pay higher taxes to help the homeless, for example. Yet George Bush was elected president and one of his most often-quoted promises was: "no new taxes."

As this country moves into the 1990s, the ongoing debate about the collection and distribution of national resources continues.

## LOOKING FORWARD

One of the greatest challenges facing the United States in the final decade of the twentieth century is that of creating opportunities for all citizens to lead the most healthy and productive lives possible. Achieving this goal could benefit not just the poor but the entire society.

Efforts continue at many different levels. Legislators—including local, state, and federal—continue to look at laws and programs to help those in need: People in private industry, education, health care, and social services contribute their resources; individuals play a vital role, too.

How can individuals make an impact on the problem of

poverty in the United States? Citizens can exercise the right to vote and can become informed about issues and candidates. They can join organizations that study and attempt to influence different problems affecting their own areas, as well as those that affect the entire nation. Many organizations inform their members about current legislation before Congress so that individuals can contact their elected representatives and voice their opinions.

There are also opportunities to respond to needs in the local community. Charitable groups, programs such as "Meals on Wheels," literacy volunteer efforts, shelters for the homeless, Big Brother and Big Sister programs, and family crisis centers are only a few of the organizations that offer chances for concerned people to help others. People can contribute time and money to these and to various national organizations.

The pastoral letter of the American Catholic bishops called upon all Americans to "take the necessary steps to ensure that no one among us is hungry, homeless, unemployed, or otherwise denied what is necessary to live in dignity...."

Through the years some progress has been made. The majority of Americans are not poor, and the plight of the poor may not be as bad as it was a hundred years ago or even fifty years ago. It is true, also, that Americans as a group are better off than the citizens of many other countries.

A significant number of Americans, however, do experience poverty and the grim problems it can entail—hunger, malnutrition, inadequate housing or no home at all, and the lack of education and health care. They may work very hard and still be unable to improve their economic conditions. They may be part of families that have experienced poverty for generations and see little hope for change in the future. They may be caught in a cycle of debilitating circumstances that keep them physically and mentally disadvantaged. Many of the poor are children, and the implications of this widespread poverty among the young is a cause for concern.

Poverty causes much human suffering and contributes to numerous other problems in the larger society. The efforts of the past have not eliminated poverty in this country. Perhaps new efforts—creative, persistent, concerted efforts—will be more successful, as the United States works to bring the "American dream" within the reach of all its citizens.

# BIBLIOGRAPHY

Addams, Jane. *Twenty Years at Hull House.* New York: New American Library, 1981.

American Friends Service Committee. "Farmers Co-operate to Succeed." *AFSC Quaker Service Bulletin* 153 (Winter 1986).

———. "Farmers, Farmworkers—The Struggle to Survive." *AFSC Quaker Service Bulletin* 156 (Winter 1987).

———. "Field Workers Teach Health on Reservations." *AFSC Quaker Service Bulletin* 157 (Spring 1987).

———. "U.N. Office Supports Migrant Rights." *AFSC Quaker Service Bulletin* 154 (Spring 1986).

Aronowitz, Stanley. *Food, Shelter, and the American Dream.* New York: Seabury Press, 1974.

Association on American Indian Affairs. *Indian Affairs* 115 (Winter 1986).

Auletta, Ken. *The Underclass.* New York: Random House, 1982.

Bagdikian, Ben H. *In the Midst of Plenty: The Poor in America.* Boston: Beacon Press, 1964.

Beard, Charles A., and Mary R. *The Beards' Basic History of the United States.* New York: Doubleday, Doran & Co., 1944.

Berlin, Ira. *Slaves without Masters: The Free Negro in the Antebellum South.* New York: Pantheon Books, 1974.

Bird, Caroline. *The Invisible Scar.* New York: David McKay Company, 1966.

Brown, Dee. *Bury My Heart at Wounded Knee.* New York: Holt, Rinehart and Winston, 1970.

Children's Defense Fund. *A Briefing Book on the Status of Children in 1988.* Washington, D.C., 1988.

Coles, Robert. *Children of Crisis*, vol. 2: *Migrants, Sharecroppers, Mountaineers.* Boston: Atlantic Monthly Press, 1971.

DeMarco, Susan, and Hightower, Jim. "You've Got to Spread It Around." *Mother Jones* (May 1988): 30–36; 56.

Eiseman, Alberta. *From Many Lands.* New York: Atheneum, 1974.

Ellis, Edward Robb. *A Nation in Torment: The Great American Depression 1929–1939.* New York: Coward McCann, 1970.

Fleming, Walter L., ed. *Documentary History of Reconstruction: Political, Military, Social, Religious, Educational, and Industrial, 1865 to 1906.* New York: McGraw-Hill, 1966.

Friedman, Milton. *Capitalism and Freedom.* Chicago: University of Chicago Press, 1962.

Friends Committee on National Legislation. "Congressional Action Agenda for Fall." *FCNL Newsletter* 506 (October 1987).

————. "Federal Support for Housing Shrinks at Crucial Time." *FCNL Newsletter* 499 (February 1987).

————. "FCNL Legislative Priorities for the 100th Congress, 1987–88." *FCNL Newsletter* 498 (January 1987).

————. "Native American Inheritance." *FCNL Newsletter* 496 (November 1986).

Galbraith, John Kenneth. *The Affluent Society.* Boston: Houghton-Mifflin Co., 1958.

————. *The Nature of Mass Poverty.* Cambridge, Mass.: Harvard University Press, 1979.

Gartner, Alan, et al. *Beyond Reagan: Alternatives for the '80s.* New York: Harper and Row, 1984.

Gibbs, Nancy R. "Grays on the Go." *Time.* 22 February 1988: 69–75.

Gilder, George. *Wealth and Poverty.* New York: Basic Books, 1981.

Harrington, Michael. *The New American Poverty.* New York: Holt, Rinehart and Winston, 1984.

————. *The Other America: Poverty in the United States.* New York: Macmillan, 1962.

Heatherly, Charles L., and Pines, Burton Yale, eds. *Mandate for Leadership III: Policy Strategies for the 1990s.* Washington, D.C.: Heritage Foundation, 1989.

Himmelfarb, Gertrude. *The Idea of Poverty.* New York: Alfred A. Knopf, 1984.

Hollyman, Stephanie. *We the Homeless.* New York: Philosophical Library, 1988.

Humphrey, Hubert. *War on Poverty.* New York: McGraw-Hill, 1964.

Hunter, Floyd. *The Big Rich and the Little Rich.* New York: Doubleday, 1965.

Kemp, Jack. *An American Renaissance.* New York: Harper and Row, 1979.

Kotz, Nick. *Let Them Eat Promises: The Politics of Hunger in America.* Englewood Cliffs, N.J.: Prentice-Hall, 1969.

Kozol, Jonathan. "The Homeless and Their Children." *The New Yorker.* 25 January 1988, 1 February 1988.

Lapham, Lewis H. *Fortune's Child.* Garden City, N.Y.: Doubleday, 1980.

Lapham, Lewis H., et al. *The Harper's Index Book.* New York: Henry Holt & Co., 1987.

League of Women Voters. *The National Voter* (April 1988).

Lens, Sidney. *Poverty: America's Enduring Paradox.* New York: Thomas Y. Crowell Company, 1969.

Letwin, William, ed. *A Documentary History of American Economic Policy Since 1789.* Garden City, N.Y.: Doubleday, 1961.

Levine, Richard. "New York's Economic Growth Fails to Curb Rise of 'New Poverty.'" *New York Times.* 28 February 1989: 1, 1.

Levitan, Sar A., and Shapiro, Isaac. *Working But Poor: America's Contradiction.* Baltimore: Johns Hopkins University Press, 1987.

Lewis, Sasha G. *Slave Trade Today: American Exploitation of Illegal Aliens.* Boston: Beacon Press, 1979.

Loebl, Eugen. *Humanomics: How We Can Make the Economy Serve Us—Not Destroy Us.* New York: Random House, 1976.

Mathews, Tom. "Homeless in America: What Can Be Done?" *Newsweek.* 21 March 1988.

Mayhew, Henry. *London Labour and the London Poor.* New York: Dover Publications, 1968.

McIntyre, Robert S. *Corporate Income Taxes in the Reagan Years.* Washington, D.C.: Citizens for Tax Justice, 1984.

McPherson, James M. *The Oxford History of the United States,* vol. 6: *Battle Cry of Freedom: The Civil War Era.* New York: Oxford University Press, 1988.

Melman, Seymour. *Our Depleted Society.* New York: Holt, Rinehart and Winston, 1965.

Midgeley, Jane. *The Women's Budget.* Philadelphia: Women's International League for Peace and Freedom, 1985.

Migrant Legal Action Program. *MEMO—Migrant Education Monthly* (March–April 1988).

———. "Farmworker Law Developments in 1988." *Clearinghouse Review* (January 1989).

Moynihan, Daniel Patrick. *The Politics of a Guaranteed Income.* New York: Random House, 1973.

Murray, Charles. *In Pursuit: Of Happiness and Good Government.* New York: Simon and Schuster, 1988.

———. *Losing Ground: American Social Policy, 1950–1980.* New York: Basic Books, 1984.

Nevins, Allan, and Commager, Henry Steele. *America, the Story of a Free People.* Boston: Little, Brown, 1943.

North, Douglass C. *Growth and Welfare in the American Past.* Englewood Cliffs, N.J.: Prentice-Hall, 1966.

Pifer, Alan, and Bronte, Diane Lydia, eds. *Our Aging Society.* New York: W. W. Norton Co., 1986.

Rosenberg, Nathan. *Technology and American Economic Growth.* White Plains, N.Y.: M. E. Sharpe, 1972.

Rothschild, Emma. *The Decline of the Auto-Industrial Age.* New York: Random House, 1973.

Samuelson, Robert J. "Beyond the Budget Fuss." *Newsweek.* 28 November 1988: 33.

Satchell, Michael. "Bent But Not Broken." *Parade.* 10 October 1982: 6–10.

Save the Children Federation. *Save the Children 1982 Annual Report. Fiftieth Anniversary Issue.* Westport, Conn., 1989.

Sowell, Thomas. *Say's Law: An Historical Analysis.* Princeton, N.J.: Princeton University Press, 1972.

Stockman, David. *The Triumph of Politics.* Harper & Row, 1986.

Thurow, Lester. *Generating Inequality.* New York: Basic Books, 1975.

Wald, Lillian. *The House on Henry Street.* New York: Dover Publications, 1971.

# INDEX

Addams, Jane, 36, 98
Agricultural Relations Board, 47
Agriculture. *See* Farms and farm
  workers
Agriculture Department, 4, 45,
  60
Aid to Families with Dependent
  Children, 33–34, 71–73, 94,
  100, 104, 110
Alcohol abuse, 54–55, 107–109
Alcoholics Anonymous, 109
American Association of Retired
  Persons, 78–79, 85
American Federation of Labor,
  18
American Friends Service
  Committee, 48–49, 54–55,
  111
American Revolution, 11–12
Appalachia, 44, 56–60
Appalachia Fireside Crafts, 60
Appalachian Regional
  Commission, 57
Area Redevelopment
  Administration, 57
Asetoyer, Charon, 54
Auletta, Ken, 59, 62
Automation, 39, 87
Automobile industry, 38, 86

Beard, Sam, 95–96
Bennett, William, 108

"Big brother" programs, 62–63,
  112
Blacks, 45, 60–64
  children, 61–62, 65
  civil rights movement, 26–27
  elderly, 6, 77
  income, 62
  legal equality, 44, 61
  unemployment, 62
  women, 6, 26, 63
  *See also* Slavery
"Bonus March" (1932), 22–23
Brock, Horace, 83–84
Brookings Institution, 21, 100
Brown, Dee, 53
Budget (U.S.)
  deficit, 41–42
  social program cuts, 33–36
*Bury My Heart at Wounded Knee*,
  53
Bush, George, 40, 41, 73, 102,
  111

CANDO (Community Area New
  Development Organization),
  58
*Capitalism and Freedom*, 35
Carter, Jimmy, 30, 106
Catastrophic Coverage Act, 81
Census Bureau, 1, 2, 4, 6–7, 32,
  52, 62, 65

Charity, 13, 26, 88, 94, 98, 112
Chavez, Cesar, 47
Child support payments, 69, 71,
    100, 101
Children, 6, 20, 112
    black, 61–62, 65
    and divorce, 69–71
    effects of poverty on, 65–67
    federal program cuts, 33–34
    health care, 51, 107
    homeless, 13, 66, 92, 95
    legislation to help, 74
    malnutrition, 33, 42, 45, 57,
        66, 106
    of migrant workers, 45, 49–51
Children of the Tenements, The, 18
Children's Defense Fund, 74–75
Cities, homeless in, 92–94
Civil Rights Acts, 14, 61
Civil rights movement, 26–27
Civil War, 13, 14, 15, 61
Civil Works Administration, 23
Civilian Conservation Corps,
    23–24
Clark, Joseph, 29
Clothing and textile industry,
    38–39, 86, 88
Coal mining, 56–57
"Comic Relief," 95
Commerce Department, 57
Conference on Economic
    Progress, 27
Coolidge, Calvin, 21
Corporate mergers, 36–37, 90
Cost-of-living adjustments, 77
Council of Economic Advisors,
    27
Crime, 13, 63, 66, 78, 92, 108,
    109

Day care, 63, 72, 73, 74
DeConcini, Dennis, 56
Defense budget, 33, 36
Dingell, John, 107
Displaced workers, 7, 40, 89–92
Divorce, 69–71
Drug abuse, 13, 92, 106–109
Dukakis, Michael, 63

Economic Opportunity Act, 28
Education
    lack of, 7, 14, 45, 53, 62, 64,
        102
    for migrant youth, 45, 49–51
    See also Job-training programs
Edwards, Don, 74
Elderly, 6, 28, 76–85, 97
Equal Rights Amendment, 74
Espinoza, Pablo, 49
Evans, George Henry, 14

Factory closings and moves,
        37–38, 40, 86, 87
Fair Labor Standards Act, 48,
    101
Fairbanks, Judy, 55
"Farm Aid," 95
Farmers Home Administration
    program, 95
Farms and farm workers
    in 1800s, 9, 14, 15, 16
    in 1920s, 20, 21
    in 1930s, 22, 24–25
    in 1980s, 86, 88–89
    elderly, 79
    as new poor, 7, 42, 66
    sharecropping, 61
    See also Migrant workers

Farmworker Labor Organizing
   Committee, 49
Federal-State Employment
   Service, 91–92
Fetal alcohol syndrome, 54–55
Food budget, 4, 5
Food and diet. *See* Hunger and
   malnutrition
Food Program for Women,
   Infants, and Children, 107
Food stamps, 33, 58, 70–71, 110
Foreign labor, 37–39, 41, 86
Frank, Barney, 94
Freedman's Act, 14
Friedman, Milton, 35
Friends Committee on National
   Legislation, 55–56, 111

Ghettos, 26, 44, 78
Gilder, George, 34–35
Giving Rural Adults a Study
   Program (GRASP), 50
Government programs, 20,
   23–31, 42, 58, 97–99, 101
Gramm-Rudman-Hollings Act,
   41
Great Depression, 21–26, 42, 43,
   94
Great Society programs, 28–29,
   58
Greeley, Horace, 13

"Habitat for Humanity," 106
Hamilton, Alexander, 12
Harrington, Michael, 4, 27, 33,
   34
Hawkins, Augustus F., 74, 101

Head Start, 28, 29, 51, 58, 63,
   74, 110
Health care, 42, 106–107
   blacks, 62
   children, 34, 51, 107
   elderly, 28, 77, 79–82
   migrant workers, 51–52
   native Americans, 53–55
   women, 34, 65–66, 73
Heritage Foundation, 100–101
Higher Education Act, 28
Hispanics, 45, 77
Homeless, 7, 13, 22, 42, 66,
   92–95, 103–106
Homestead Act, 14, 15
Hoover, Herbert, 21, 22
Hopkins, Harry L., 23
Housing, 5, 7, 35, 62, 77–79,
   92, 94, 103–106
   *See also* Homeless
Housing Assistance Council,
   78–79
Housing and Urban
   Development program, 73,
   78
*How the Other Half Lives*, 18
Humphrey, Hubert, 28, 57
Hunger and malnutrition, 7, 22,
   42, 53, 57, 58, 62, 66, 106
Hunter, Robert, 18

Illiteracy, 14, 53, 73, 102
Immigrants, 13, 18, 44
Imported goods, 41, 86
Indentured servants, 8–9
Indian Health Service, 54
Indian Reorganization Act, 53
Indians, *See* Native Americans

Industrial Revolution, 12, 43
Industrial workers, 7, 68, 86–88
Inflation, 30, 33, 35, 36, 41
Interest rates, 33, 35, 41

Jackson, Jesse, 35–36, 63, 85
Jefferson, Thomas, 11, 12
Job market, 38–41
Job-Training Partnership Act, 91
Job-training programs, 28, 91,
    100, 101–103, 109–110
Johnson, Lyndon B., 28, 58
"Jubilee Housing," 106

Kemp, Jack, 73
Kennedy, Edward, 35–36
Kennedy, John F., 27–28, 57
Kennedy, Joseph, 104
Kennedy, Robert F., 29
Kildee, Dale E., 74
King, Martin Luther, Jr., 27
Koch, Edward, 108
Kozol, Jonathan, 104

Labor Department, 22, 68–69
Legal aid, 49
Levitan, Sar A., 44–45
Lewis, Oscar, 6
Lopez, Benito, 48

Malnutrition. *See* hunger and
    malnutrition
MDRC (Manpower Demonstra-
    tion Research Corporation),
    59–60, 63
Meals on Wheels, 112
Medicaid, 34, 73

Medicare, 28, 77, 79–82
Mentally ill, 92
Migrant Dropout Reconnection
    Program, 50
Migrant Education Fund, 50
Migrant Legal Action Program,
    45, 48
Migrant and Seasonal
    Agricultural Worker
    Protection Act, 48
Migrant Student Transfer
    System, 50
Migrant workers, 45–56
Mikulski, Barbara, 110
Minimum wage, 101
Moynihan, Daniel P., 99–100
Murray, Charles, 35

Nader, Ralph, 35–36
National Association of State
    Boards of Education,
    102–103
National Coalition for the
    Homeless, The, 7, 92
National Commission of Jobs
    and Small Businesses, 40,
    95
National Council of Catholic
    Bishops, 32, 111, 112
National Council of *La Raza*, 77
National debt, 41
National Employee
    Homeownership Program,
    106
National Industrial Recovery
    Act, 24
National Low Income Housing
    Coalition Partnership Act,
    104

National Organization for Women, 74
National Reform Association, 14
National service, proposals, 109–110
Native Americans, 45, 52–56
*New American Poverty, The*, 4, 33
New Deal, 23–26
New Jersey low-income housing, 105
"New poor," 7, 86–96
Nixon, Richard, 53
Nunn, Sam, 109

Occupational hazards, 18, 47–50, 56–57
Office of Indian Education, 56
Older Farmworkers Housing Project, 79
Organization for Unemployment Relief, 22
*Other America, The*, 4, 27

Peterson, Peter, 85
Physicians' Task Force on Hunger in America, 42, 106
Populist movement, 16
Poverty
    challenges for 1990s, 97–113
    chronic, 44–64
    current, 32–43
    definitions, 5–7
    in Great Depression, 21–26
    measuring, 2–5
    "new," 7, 86–96
    in 1920s, 20–21

past government policies, 20, 23–31
in pre-twentieth century, 8–16
rate increase, 6, 7, 32, 96
rural, 88–89
in twentieth century, 17–31
war on, 26–31, 61, 77
*Poverty in the United Kingdom*, 5
Prison inmates, 108–109
Public Works Administration, 23

Quakers, 10–11

Railroads, 15–16
Reagan administration, 33–40
Reagan, Ronald, 30–31
Reischauer, Robert, 100
Riis, Jacob, 18
Roosevelt, Franklin D., 23
Roosevelt, Theodore, 18, 20
Rouse, James, 106
Roybal, Edward, 85
Rural areas, 88–89
    *See also* Farms and farm workers

Save the Children Federation, 60
School lunch program, 33
Schumer, Charles, 94, 104
Service industry, 40, 86, 87
Settlement houses, 98
Shapiro, Isaac, 44–45
Shelters and welfare hotels, 93, 94, 104, 112
Single-parent families, 65, 66, 69–71
Slavery, 9–10, 12, 14, 61, 64

Slums, 18, 26, 44, 78
Small businesses, 89–91
Snowe, Olympia J., 74
Social Security, 6, 77, 82–85
Social Security Act, 25, 82
Solomon, Gerald B., 85
Soup kitchens, 22, 42, 53–54, 93
Steel industry, 86, 88
Steffens, Lincoln, 18
Stevens, Thaddeus, 14
Stockman, David, 34, 35
Strikes, 18, 24
Supplemental Security Income,
    83
Supportive Housing
    Demonstration, 95
Sweatshops, 18


Taxes, 30, 35, 36, 41
Technology industry, 40
Teenage pregnancy, 72, 100
Textile industry. *See* Clothing
    and textile industry.
Townsend, Peter, 5
Trade Adjustment Assistance
    program, 91
Trade deficit, 41


*Underclass, The*, 59, 62
Unemployment, 17, 30, 33, 40,
    42, 52, 64, 66, 87, 92,
    109–110
Unions, 88
United Farm Workers Union, 47
United Migrant Association, 48

United Way, 98


Vento, Bruce F., 73–74, 94
VISTA (Volunteers in Service to
    America), 58
Vocational training. *See* Job-
    training programs
Voting Rights Act, 61


Wages, 6, 33, 62, 101
War on poverty, 26–31, 61, 77
*War on Poverty*, 57
*Wealth and Poverty*, 34
Weiss, Ted, 94
Welfare hotels. *See* Shelters and
    welfare hotels
Welfare programs, 33–35, 42,
    71–73, 110-111
Welfare reform, 99–101, 102
Wilson, Woodrow, 20
Women, 6, 13, 18, 20, 26,
    65–75, 100
  elderly, 77
  legal rights of, 67
  native American, 54–55
"Women of All Red Nations," 55
Women's International League
    for Peace and Freedom, 36,
    111
Works Progress Administration,
    25
World War I, 18, 20, 22–23
World War II, 25, 26, 68, 84


Youth employment, 109–110